Flowerkeeping

Flowerkeeping

The Time-Honored Art of Preserving Flowers

Written by Georgeanne Brennan
Photography by Kathryn Kleinman
Crafts by Teresa Retzlaff

Ten Speed Press
Berkeley, California

For Teresa,

with many thanks

K.K. & G.B.

Ten Speed Press
Box 7123
Berkeley, California 94707
A Kirsty Melville Book

Distributed in Australia by Simon and Schuster Australia, in Canada by Ten Speed Press Canada,
in New Zealand by Southern Publishers Group, in South Africa by Real Books, in Southeast Asia by
Berkeley Books, and in the United Kingdom and Europe by Airlift Books.

Craft concepts and production by Teresa Retzlaff.
Additional craft production and styling by Sarah Dawson (cover; pp. 97, 99)
and Michaele Thunen (pp. 73, 133, 134).
Photography assistants: Caroline Kopp and Anthony Gamboa.
Cover and text design by Gretchen Scoble.
Copyediting by Sharon Silva.

Library of Congress Cataloging-in-Publication Data on file with the publisher.

Printed in Hong Kong
First printing, 1999

1 2 3 4 5 6 7 8 9 10 — 03 02 01 00 99

This Book Belongs to

ɛɔ

TABLE OF CONTENTS

Keeping

Flowerkeeping, although most commonly thought of as pressing flowers as keepsakes, is used in this book in its broadest sense. It encompasses the entire range of preserving flowers, leaves, moss, vines, and even fruits and vegetables. Whether gathered from the wild or garden grown, hothouse, or field grown, the bounty of the natural world is at our fingertips. We can bring it into our homes using the simplest of preserving techniques, from sand-, silica-, air-, or freeze-drying to pressing or waxing. Such methods are neither time consuming nor difficult, even for the novice. Then, to go a step further, we can use what we have preserved to create simple yet extraordinary wreaths, table decorations, wall hangings, decorative boxes, picture frames, and gift wraps. The only limit is our imagination.

*T*HE PAST IS BOTH AN INSPIRATION AND A TEACHER. THE TALES OF THE TIMES and the people for whom flowers were a part of daily life in their gardens, in collections, and in simple home crafts brings greater meaning to our efforts today. A few of these stories are told in this book. We can go back to the eighteenth and nineteenth centuries, when the early breeders of flowers such as pansies, dahlias, peonies, and tulips were as celebrated for their successes as movie stars are today. The public avidly followed the daring exploits of plant collectors who went into the wilds and brought back previously unknown species for the breeders. Home and estate gardeners experimented with growing the new introductions, perusing plant catalogs and garden shows to make their choices.

At that time, flowers, vines, fruits, nuts, and vegetables, both fresh and dried, were an extremely important part of home and personal adornment. Wreaths, swags, and garlands were not only popular decorations for front doors, gates, and windows, but also for dresses, hats, and shawls. Floral table decorations were important as well and included candles, wreaths, and place cards. Shortly after being welcomed to a home, visitors were commonly shown a folio of pressed flowers or a display case of collected natural finds.

In this book, we look both backward and forward, finding in our gardens, woods, and natural surroundings the same elements our predecessors found, elements that encourage us all to participate in the process of preserving as a means of creating beautiful ways to keep flowers with us, even though we may lead busy and hurried lives. It takes little time to preserve flowers and to use them in simple crafts, activities we can share with our children, passing on to them the pleasures of preserving nature.

In the past, certain flowers and plants were cultivated specifically with the intent of drying them for ornamentation. This was the case in western Europe and the United States in both the great estate gardens of the nineteenth and early twentieth centuries and in the small pleasure gardens of the middle-class homeowner of the same period. Other flowers were planted primarily for cut flowers, but were then dried as well, either by design or chance.

During the Victorian period, any sizable English estate or manor house had extensive gardens and a garden staff to oversee every aspect of the grounds, hothouses, orchards, and kitchen garden. The cutting flowers were planted in the kitchen garden, alongside the rows of beans, beets, and chard. The everlasting flowers—those grown to be dried—were planted in the cutting garden as well. The estate's demand for cut flowers to supply both the town house and the country house was so enormous that William Robinson, the notable English garden journalist of the late nineteenth century, remarked that the cutting flower gardens, like the estate's kitchen gardens, needed to be managed like a production market garden. Production gardens, unlike pleasure gardens, must first of all produce a certain volume on a regular schedule throughout the growing season. Because the growing season for fresh-cut flowers ended with the frosts of winter, it was les immortelles, varieties of flowers grown

specifically to be dried, that were used to compose *bouquets d'hiver*—the arrangements of dried flowers that ornamented houses during the winter. The same flowers were used to decorate tables, place cards, and to make swags and wreaths. The English adapted the French terms into everyday usage.

Not surprisingly, the local seedsmen played a key role during this period. Each community had at least one seed shop and larger towns had several. The seeds were kept in banks of wooden drawers or hoppers lined with tin to protect them from insect damage. Both home gardeners and estate gardeners went to the shops for their seeds, which would be scooped out of the drawers, weighed, and put in little bags or wrapped in paper parcels.

Vilmorin-Andrieux was one such shop in Paris. Similar seed shops existed in London and the other major cities of Europe, but as times changed and the cities engulfed the surrounding rural areas, many of the seed shops closed or moved, following their agricultural clients.

In spring, when seeds and seedlings were planted for summer's and fall's cut flowers, seeds were also planted to produce dried flowers for winter, when only hothouse-grown blooms would otherwise be available. Helichrysum in shades of carmine, violet, and cream, Cupid's dart in blue and silver, and sea lavender were among the flowers that were commonly planted in the kitchen garden and provided orderly and attractive borders of summer color until harvested and taken to the drying rooms to be hung and dried. Among the flowers picked from the garden grounds and dried were roses, hydrangeas, and the newly popular pansies. Unlike the flowers from the production garden, however, the random collection of pansies and roses to be dried was likely the handiwork of one of the members of the household, rather than of the garden staff.

Those of the middle class who had the luxury of owning land that did not need to be economically productive had landscaped grounds, pleasure gardens, and kitchen and cutting flower gardens, as the upper classes did, albeit on a smaller scale. Informed and fascinated by the popular press,

SEEDSMEN OF THE NINETEENTH CENTURY

❧

Dozens of varieties of les immortelles, the flowers grown specifically for drying, were offered by seedsmen of the nineteenth century, a testimony to the importance of dried flowers. For example, in 1883, the French seed company Vilmorin-Andrieux listed eighteen different colors and types of helichrysum, two of acroclinium, five of globe amaranth, three of pearly everlasting, and fifteen different varieties of sea lavender. The seeds, as well as plants, were sold in the Vilmorin-Andrieux seed shop in Paris on the Quai de la Mégisserie along the Seine, where it had been established since 1745. It is still there today, called simply Vilmorin.

Vilmorin-Andrieux offered an enticing artistic representation of their flowers and vegetables in a collection of lavish, original watercolors displayed in large, leatherbound folios. The watercolors, which were painted between 1877 and 1893 by several different artists who were brought to the seed company's growing grounds in Verrieres, southwest of Paris, were available for perusal in the seed shop to help customers make their choices.

which was writing about global explorers who brought exotic plants back to the Royal Botanic Gardens at Kew and elsewhere, the middle class were also enthusiastic supporters of the floral exhibitions and competitions that flourished during the nineteenth and early twentieth centuries. The middle classes, too, grew flowers that could be easily dried for *bouquets d'hiver,* fancied the latest roses, and even tried their hands at hybridizing to create new roses themselves. They filled garden spaces with the latest in bedding plants, ornamental shrubs, and whatever exotica they could grow. The upper classes of course, with their grand estates employing gardening staffs of hundreds, were able to have not only the elaborate gardens, but also the supporting infrastructures of hothouses, cold frames, conservatories, and glasshouses.

Few of us today have estates or gardening assistance, but many of us have gardens or a bit of ground where we would like to have a garden, or even a window box. We can purchase many of the same seeds that the estate and amateur gardeners of the nineteenth century purchased, plus hundreds more. Happily, many of the older strains, now called heirlooms, have been either maintained or reintroduced by seed companies, so that we can grow some of the larkspurs, rudbeckias, helichrysum, sweet peas, and dahlias that the Victorians grew. Although few of the seed strains for many of the pansy and violet varieties that were grown a hundred years ago are still available commercially, there have been numerous new varieties developed that give us a great array from which to choose.

Many favorite cutting flowers, bedding flowers, and flowering landscape shrubs are as enticing dried as they are fresh. Lush peonies, multi- or single-petaled, make exceptional dried flowers, and their shape is readily maintained when they are dried in silica sand. Hydrangeas were very popular in nineteenth-century gardens and are highly regarded today, both fresh and dried. They are an excellent choice for all forms of preserving. Tulips, daffodils, and narcissuses, which are rarely thought of as dried flowers, make excellent subjects, especially the less common species tulips that are tiny and unusually shaped.

Wild places were another source for flowers to dry for decorations. It was considered quite important to bring back flowers, leaves, seedpods, and bits of moss or lichen as souvenirs of travels and excursions into nature. During the Victorian era, travelers pressed and put into albums such flowers as blue gentian picked during a summer walk in an alpine meadow or a fragrant sprig of flowering rosemary gathered from a stroll along a hillside above the Mediterranean Sea. Once home, the albums, often annotated, were displayed and, like photographs, provoked drawing room reminiscing and conversations about the scenery, events, and people that had comprised the excursion. Dried berries, nuts, and seedpods, along with seashells or pebbles that might have been gathered during one's travels, were arranged into collections and showcased on tabletops or inside specially constructed glass-topped, glass-sided tables.

Sometimes the flowers or pods preserved were not from a trip, but from a special occasion. Violets, rosebuds, orchids, and multihued autumn leaves were commonly tucked between the pages of a book, where they were kept as mementos of a dance, dinner, or a night at the theater.

In a more disciplined fashion than the pleasure traveler, but with equal intensity and enthusiasm, amateur and professional botanists of the nineteenth century collected and recorded plant life for scientific purposes. Men and women roamed the globe gathering flowers, grasses, and plant specimens of all kinds. Pressed, and then carefully mounted and labeled on folio pages, their findings became important records of the plant kingdom. These old folios, or herbaria, now seem to me like works of art. The angular or curving forms of plants, long since dried, their once brilliant colors now turned to sepia, beige, muted rose, and rust, have the added element of being a physical link to another time and place, and it is not difficult to re-create this look. Pressed and mounted on fine paper, labeled, and framed, perhaps in groups of three or four, they bring grace to a room, as well as a memory of collecting the plant and the personal process of preserving it.

But pausing on a trail or a roadside to pick up a seedpod or an early spring flower that catches one's fancy is not an exercise that ended with the Victorian age, nor did the amateur collecting of plant specimens. Many of us made our own early collections of pressed plants. I remember mine quite clearly. It had a bright green posterboard cover, black scrapbook pages, and was laced together with black yarn. Inside were carefully pressed samples of the grasses and flowers that grew in the vacant lots in my neighborhood, as well as a few that I collected from the nearby hills or from the edges of the beach a few blocks away. In my very best ninth-grade handwriting I wrote out both the common and Latin names on little white labels that I glued next to the pressed plants. My friend's son, only nine years old, recently completed the same project for his school class, and keeps his plant album proudly displayed in the living room.

Walks and rambles continue to yield gathered flowers and grasses, if not for pressing, then for bouquets. The first wild oats, still tinged with green, a lacy stem of Queen Anne's lace, or long-stemmed pods left behind by wild poppies are all good candidates for gathering, as are mosses with or without bark. Like many of us, I often bring home a bit of nature, either absentmindedly or intentionally.

It is almost impossible for me to be in a forest without bringing home a swatch of moss. As a child, my mother regaled me with fairy tales and fantasies in which what the fairies were wearing and how their homes were furnished were as important to the story as the adventures and misadventures of the characters. Sleeping fairies and elves were depicted lying tucked beneath fluffy moss blankets dotted with tiny blossoms of wood hyacinth. The castle floors of knighted muskrats and warrens of dashing rabbit princes were made snug with carpets of tufted, emerald green moss, smooth to the touch like velvet, and the cottage windows of homely little field mice were hung with gossamer Spanish moss neatly tied back with twists of wild grapevine.

LOVE·IN·A·MIST

NIGELLA DAMASCENA

ALL SELF SOWN THIS YEAR - BLUE & WHITE MIXED.
(MORE BLUE). MOSTLY IN THE BED BY THE GREEN
GARAGE - LESS SUN? BEGAN BLOOMING EARLY MARCH,
THROUGH LATE JUNE. THEY WERE VERY PROLIFIC,
I LEFT THEM UNTIL THE SEED PODS FORMED, THEN
CUT THEM TO HANG & DRY. TIP: DON'T CUT THE PODS
TOO EARLY, WAIT UNTIL THEY ARE PRETTY MUCH DRY.
TOO SOON, AND THEY SHRIVEL UP. ALSO, LEFT IN THE
GARDEN LONGER THEY WILL SOW FOR NEXT YEAR.

Gathered from the forest, meadow, or roadside, cut from gardens large or small, grand and imposing or simple and unprepossessing, preserved flowers have a place in our lives today as much as they did in the lives of people who have gone before us. Ferns or flowers frozen in ice for a single night to make a bucket for Champagne, long canes of rose hips twisted into a simple wreath to last the winter season, a picture frame of pressed flowers, a centerpiece of waxed fruits for the holidays—all are ways that the simple art of flowerkeeping fits into everyday life.

It is our hope that this book will inspire you to create your own dried flower crafts, as well as to follow the instructions for those that have been included. Preserving flowers and using them in the crafts and decorations explained here is extremely easy and generally quite quick to do. Waxing, freezing, air-drying, silica-drying, sugaring, and pressing of flowers take very little time and effort, yet the process and the end result are both immensely rewarding.

CHAPTER 1

Air-Drying

The simplest way to preserve flowers and other plants is by air-drying, and air-dried blossoms, fruits, pods, grasses, and vines can be readily incorporated into decorative elements with little or no further treatment. Bunches of dried red roses, hung upside down near a doorway with a ribbon, are a reminder of a gift received or of an abundant garden. Dried peonies, autumn leaves, or rose petals scattered across a cloth-covered dinner table are a lovely—and easy—decoration. A bowlful of collected acorns and seed-pods mixed with a stem or two of dried hydrangea is a handsome coffee-table centerpiece. We especially like bowls of dried fruits such as pomegranates, limes, and oranges combined with walnuts, almonds, and a few dried leaves, along with a nutcracker. Tall grasses can be arranged in large, upright baskets or ceramic jars to fill a corner space. Freshly cut vines or shrubs can be woven or twisted into wreaths before being dried, to give them an animated appearance.

To AIR-DRY THE HARVESTED FLOWERS, GRASSES, OR OTHER PLANTS, PLACE THEM IN a warm, dry environment with adequate air circulation and allow their moisture to evaporate. Air temperatures for drying can range from 50 degrees Fahrenheit to 120 degrees Fahrenheit, but in all instances there should be enough air circulation to remove the moisture that the heat extracts. This will prevent mold from setting in before drying is complete. For maximum color retention, the drying location should be dark, since light causes the plants' pigments to break down. If muted earth tones such as buff and brown are acceptable, darkness is not a concern.

There are three main air-drying techniques: hang-drying, flat-drying, and upright-drying. The choice of technique depends in part upon the growth habit of the plant and in part upon the desired final effect. Hang-drying yields straight stems and precisely positioned flower heads, and it can used for most kinds of flowers and grasses. Long-stemmed hang-dried flowers and grasses are especially suitable for arranging in bouquets in vases or other containers or for hanging as decoration. For example, wires can be stretched from one wall to another in a room, and then hung with bunches of dried roses in shades of red, yellow, orange, and pink; larkspurs in blue, white, and pink, deep yellow yarrow; and helichrysum in a riot of colors. You can cover the whole ceiling with flowers, or maybe just string up a row or two.

HANG-DRYING There are several principles to keep in mind when hang-drying. Plants should be freshly gathered and free of excess moisture. The leaves should be stripped from flower stems if they will interfere with air circulation, or mold may develop after bunching. If you want to keep the leaves, hang the stems singly. The number of stems per bunch will depend upon the type of flower, grass, or herb you are drying. Small-flowered, thin-stemmed varieties, such as lavender and larkspur, can be gathered into bigger bunches than large-flowered or thick-stemmed ones. In any case, gather your stems into bunches no larger than a loose handful and bind the stems together with an elastic band or tightly wrapped string or cord. As the stems dry they will shrink, and if they are not tightly bound, they will slip apart. The bunches are generally hung suspended from wire or from drying racks in a warm, dark, dry place such as a large closet or an attic where they will be safe from direct sunlight.

The actual amount of time needed to complete drying depends upon the type of plant and the local temperature and humidity. It may take only a few days for a five-stem bunch of roses to dry, but two weeks may be needed for a three-stem bunch of large alliums. Thinner-stemmed, lightly petaled flowers dry more quickly than those with a high moisture and fiber content such as sunflowers.

The best natural conditions for hang-drying occur during summer, although in many areas, summers can also be quite humid. If humidity is high, it is especially important to keep air circulation high, perhaps by temporarily installing a fan in your drying space and leaving a moist air exit.

Once dried, the hanging bunches can be left in place until you are ready to use them, or they can be removed, wrapped carefully in paper, and stored in covered cardboard boxes. The boxes should be kept in a dry, insect-free environment.

FLAT-DRYING Flat-drying on racks is particularly suited for thick, fleshy sunflower heads, for heads of heavily petaled, dense flowers such as cactus dahlias and beehive zinnias, and also for stemmed flowers where asymmetry and curves are sought, such as sweet-pea vines and old-fashioned clustered garden roses. Picked green, flower, nut, and tree pods are best dried on racks, as are such hard-skinned fruits as oranges and pomegranates. Dried sunflowers or zinnias, balanced on their stems, can be lined up across a mantel. They can also be dried for bouquets, wreaths, or to decorate a package. Since the heads can be heavy and the hollow stems have been weakened with drying, it's a good idea to replace the natural stems with wire stems made by running the wire through the calyx (the thick part of the flower head base), and then twisting it together. Because of the fragility of dried flowers, wiring is best done before drying to avoid overhandling. Stemless heads can be used as simple table decorations.

Since the flower heads will be flattened on one side if simply laid flat on a rack, it is best to stick them through the wire or mesh to hold them upright. First trim them to a short stem length, remove the stem just below the green calyx, or make an artificial stem as explained above. Insert the natural or wire stem through a hole in the screen or mesh, with the flower head facing upward and resting on the surface. Place stemless flowers on the rack, face upward. Place vegetables and fruits such as gourds, winter squashes, oranges, and pomegranates and large pods like those of wisteria directly on the rack and turn occasionally. Use racks to dry branches of leaves such as magnolia or maple, where a bit of curl in the leaf is desirable, and vines. Grapevines and sweet-pea vines can first be twisted into wreathlike shapes and then left to dry flat.

Light petals such as those of tulips, roses, peonies, and other large petals, as well as whole flower heads of the papery-petaled narcissus and daffodil, can be flat-dried on trays or between sheets of folded newspaper. Branches, grasses, and foliage that are already semidry can be placed between folded sheets of newspaper and laid flat in layers to finish the drying process. The dried petals crinkle and curl beneath the paper, drying naturally but retaining their color because they are out of the light. Once dried, keep the petals in glass jars, put them in the bases of clear glass lamps, or leave them in attractive bowls. Fragrant petals can be made into sachets.

UPRIGHT-DRYING Some grasses, such as headed wheat and rice and other nearly dry plants like curly dock and cattails, can be dried by simply by placing them upright in containers with no further treatment. Upright-drying in evaporating water, a technique that achieves a natural curving or nodding appearance, is done by placing the stemmed flowers upright in containers with a few inches of water. As the water evaporates the flowers dry slowly and naturally, yet without wilting. This works well for such flowers as rose bouquets, single-petaled zinnias, and hydrangeas.

GARDEN-DRYING Another method of air-drying is to leave flowers and other plants growing in the garden to dry naturally as they near the end of their growing season, begin to develop seeds, and die down. This method is only successful in warm, dry climates, but spectacular results can be achieved. Consider a towering hollyhock entwined with morning glory vines, dried to a creamy buff, its leaves long gone, but the shiny, deep red seedpods still intact. Or picture equally tall stalks of corn wound with the vines and pods of the climbing beans they supported, a ready-made decoration for autumn. You only need to cut the stalk and the vine.

Plants may be also be cut or uprooted and then hung or spread outside to dry. If kept sheltered, they will retain their color. Many fruits and vegetables are dried this way, including chiles, grapes, figs, and beans. Chiles can be dried on strings, or *ristras:* thread a large, sharp needle with a long piece of heavy-duty button thread, double and knot it, and then pierce the top of each pepper through the thickest and strongest part of the green calyx. Continue the threading until only about 6 inches of the thread remains, then cut off the needle and tie the ends of the thread, and hang the chiles to dry. They can be dried indoors as well, in the same manner as hang-dried flowers.

Be forewarned, though, that plants left outside to dry, whether still in the garden or cut and hung, are more likely to be prey to pests than those kept inside. If nights and mornings are moist, it is better to bring the drying plants inside a shed or other area to protect them. They can then be put outside the next day in the warm sun.

OVEN-DRYING Oven-drying is quick and simple and results in a truly sumptuous potpourri of colors, shapes, and scents. Flowers, leaves, and some thinly sliced fruits may be dried in an oven set between 175 and 200 degrees Fahrenheit. Single petals and many leaves are most suitable for this treatment, as they dry more quickly than heavy-petaled, full flower heads which are prone to the petals crisping before the heavier center is fully dried. If your are set on oven-drying larger heads, consider starting the drying process in the oven and finish air-drying them on racks.

Tulip petals, especially those of the large, flamboyant parrot tulips make beautiful and unusual dried petals. Simply gather the petals as they fall, either in the garden or from a vase indoors, then spread the petals on a baking sheet and put them in a preheated oven just long enough to dry, about 20 minutes. Once done, store the petals in a paper bag, glass jar, or tin until you are ready to use them, where they will keep for six months or more in a dry location.

Rose petals can be dried in the same way. If you have access to some of the ultrafragrant old roses such as the bright pink *Rosa rugosa,* 'Rubra', purple-hued hybrid perpetual 'Reine de Violettes', or the magenta moss rose, 'William Lobb', oven-dry them. The colors remain intense and the fragrance intact, so that they make a complete component in a potpourri.

Other fragrant choices for oven-drying are sage leaves, lemon verbena, and mint. Any variety of sage can be oven-dried, including the colorful golden sage, purple sage, and tricolor. Like roses and tulips, they will retain their color. Spread the leaves on a baking sheet and put them in an oven preheated to 175 degrees Fahrenheit for about 30 minutes, checking the leaves after 10 minutes to make sure they are not burning. After 15 minutes, turn the leaves. They are done when they feel papery to the touch but are not yet brittle. Remove them from the oven to cool, then place them in a paper bag, glass jar, or tin and store in a cool, dry place for six months or longer. Treat other leaves and flowers the same way, remembering the thinner and more delicate they are, the less time they will need to dry.

HARVESTING FOR AIR-DRYING The timing of the harvest is an important consideration when air-drying flowers and other plants. If harvested too early, the flowers may be limp and look wan when dried, yet if harvested too late the petals or leaves may fall after drying, leaving only stems or seed heads. Although there is some leeway, each type of flower has its optimum moment, especially important in commercial dried-flower production. Since most commercially dried flowers and plants will be boxed, shipped, and stored, then perhaps shipped again, and finally composed into arrangements, harvesting correctly maximizes sturdiness and lessens the risk of an inferior product. If you are shopping for dried flowers, rather than drying them yourself, make sure the flowers don't drop their petals when shaken slightly, the leaves are intact, and the colors are vibrant, all indicators of timely harvest and good handling.

In your own garden, a general rule of thumb for most types of blooms it that they should be harvested when one-half to three-quarters open. There are, of course, exceptions. Acroclinium, sometimes called straw-flower, must be harvested only after the flowers are fully opened and their round, bright yellow centers fully visible.

Grasses are more forgiving than flowers and can be harvested over a large maturity range. They can be cut and brought inside to dry when they are still green and before the seed heads have formed, later when the seeds heads have formed and the grasses are turning gold, or at any time in between.

Whole seedpods gathered from the garden, such as tulip, iris, wisteria, poppy, radish, and okra, may be harvested while the pods are still green yet firm to the touch and brought inside to be rack-dried, where they will retain their greenish cast. Alternatively, they may be left longer in the garden to harden and turn to beige-green. Unless you live in a dry climate, however, you will run the risk of the drying pods being rained upon, then becoming stained, broken, or moldy before they can dry out completely. Burst pods, their seeds dropped and scattered, may be harvested at any time, although they may be damaged by long exposure to the elements.

When gathering anything from the wild, whether dried pods, grasses, shrubs, or flowers, never strip a species from a site, as it will upset the natural balance. Indeed, attempt to disturb the ecosystems of any environment as little as possible. Also, never undertake gathering on any property without authorization from the owner.

Lavender

Although virtually any flower or grass can be air-dried, certain ones are especially notable, not only for the flower itself, but because of its horticultural history and the many decorative and other uses it has been put to over the years. Lavender is one of the best-known dried flowers, and because of its haunting and intense fragrance it has a long history of preservation.

Today we think of countless cultivated lavender fields as synonymous with Provence, but lavender was originally gathered wild from the hillsides and was not a cultivated crop until after World War I. Now in Provence, *touffes* of gray-green foliage and spikes of glowing lavender flowers cover several thousand acres in undulating rows over plateaus and across the flanks of steep hillsides. Of the various varieties of cultivated lavender, the one most frequently grown in France for commercial production is lavandin, the result of the spontaneous hybridization in the wild of two different lavenders, *Lavandula angustifolia* (also called *L. vera* and *L. officinalis)* and *L. latifolia.*

Lavandin was discovered at the end of the nineteenth century by gatherers who were cutting the wild lavender and noticed some plants that were considerably larger than others, with longer flower stems and more flowers. In 1927, a laboratory analysis determined that this *grosse*, or big, lavender, as it was called, was indeed a new type, a hybrid created in the wild. These larger plants were more productive than either *L. angustifolia* or *L. latifolia,* and by 1975 almost all of the commercial plantings in France were of one of three main selections of lavandin. Because hybrids do not grow true from seed, lavandin is produced by vegetative propagation, with

LAVENDER HARVEST IN PROVENCE A CENTURY AGO

❧

At the end of the nineteenth century and into the beginning of the twentieth, each summer families and extended families left their village or farm and went to the mountains to cut lavender. Arriving near dawn, before the stars had disappeared, they started cutting the wild lavender with hand sickles. A big cloth, called an apron, was laid out and the cut lavender piled into it until the four corners of the cloth could just barely be brought up over the harvest to be tied in a knot. The lavender was priced and sold by the "apron-bundle." The harvest lasted a week or more, and those who were the main cutters slept out in a stone shepherd's hut or barn, while others ferried the lavender bundles down from the hills to the distillery and brought food and other supplies back up.

Although lavandin is the primary commercial lavender in France, it can be purchased in the United States as well. The intensely fragrant, very hardy L. angustifolia, probably remains the most widely grown lavender here. It is the lavender I grow at home in California, and it makes wonderful dried flowers, full of resinous, long-lasting fragrance. I sell some of it to the wholesale fresh flower market, but most of it is purchased by buyers who hang it to dry themselves.

cuttings from a parent plant stuck into a planting medium until roots begin to sprout. Some farmers and home gardeners do their own cutting and rooting, and others buy the plants from nurseries, with the farmers buying from operations that specialize in lavandin. The rooted plants are then transplanted to the fields or to the home garden or containers.

The lavender fields of Provence are machine harvested during July, and the yield is used primarily for the perfume industry. The loose, deep purple flower spikes are loaded into large trucks that trundle back and forth from the fields to the distilleries. As they pass through the villages of the south, they leave behind them an intense aroma trail that can last several hours. Some lavender for the fresh and dried flower market is still cut by hand, as it was a hundred years ago.

Drying Lavender

It is important to harvest lavender when the flowers are in the bud stage. If it is cut later, after the flowers have opened, they will drop off during drying. For the most efficient drying, strip the leaves from the stems and gather the lavender into bundles of 30 to 50 stems, fastening them with a rubber band or tightly fastened twine. Attach a wire or other fastener to the bundles and hang them upside down at least 6 inches apart on a drying rack or a wire strung across a room to ensure adequate air circulation.

If your summer climate is hot and dry, try leaving some of the fragrant foliage attached and make thick haystacks of bundles tied with raffia or heavy cord. The bunches must be tied loosely enough to allow ample air circulation, otherwise, the leaf and stem mass will heat up and mold will grow. Hang them upside down to dry, spacing them about 1 foot apart. Once the lavender has dried, the raffia or cord can be tightened to make a snug bundle.

Lavender Wand Sachets

Ribbon-tied bundles of lavender stems, a Provencal tradition, make unusual and fragrant sachets to tuck into drawers or linen closets. To make lavender wands, gather together 39 long stems of freshly cut lavender in the bud stage. The stems must be very supple, so it is better if the lavender has been recently watered, as the stems will be softer and less likely to break during the forming of the wand. Remove the leaves and any side shoots. Cut a 2½-foot length of ¼- to ⅜-inch-wide ribbon. Gather the stems together and tightly tie the ribbon around them, just beneath the flowers. Turn the bundle flower-end down and carefully bend the stems down over the flowers one at a time. Now, weave the wand by pulling the ribbon through the stems, passing it over the first 3 stems and under the next 3. Continue until all the stems are woven. On the next row, reverse the pattern, weaving under the first 3, over the next, and so on. Continue this weaving, pulling the ribbon tight each time, and reversing the pattern on each row, until you reach the bottom of the flowers. Wrap the ribbon tightly around the stems several times at the base of the weave. Pull the end of the ribbon through the middle of the stems, then trim it to about 3 inches long. Cut another 18-inch-length of the ribbon and wrap it over the existing ribbon at the base, tying it off in a bow. Using clippers or garden scissors, trim the ends so they are all the same length. If you don't want to do the weaving, a simpler wand can be made by carefully bending the stems down over the flowers one at time, as above. When they are all bent, tightly wrap the stems just beneath the flowers with a ribbon, as above. (Because the petals are kept securely inside the folded stems, they will not spill out into the drawer and onto your clothes.)

Hydrangeas

On the list of a flower arranger's favorite specimens, hydrangeas, both fresh and dried, rank high because of their color, airy heads packed with florets, and longevity. Colors range from deepest blue, nearly violet, and deep rose pink to white and mauvish bronze, and the blossoms' light and airy forms look wonderful tucked into table settings, where the glasses will catch their reflection. The flower clusters may contain both fertile and sterile flowers, which are of different shapes. Sterile flowers are large with petal-like sepals, while fertile flowers are quite small and star shaped. Lace-cap hydrangea, an especially popular type, has a central cluster of tiny fertile flowers surrounded by a mass of larger sterile ones. There are many species of hydrangea, each with its particular characteristics. Some are climbers, such as *Hydrangea anomala,* which bears a white lace-cap-like flower, and others are large shrubs, like the garden hydrangea, *H. macrophylla,* which can grow as tall as twelve feet tall and is available in shades of blue, pink, and white. Hydrangeas bear pink and red flowers when grown in alkaline soils and blue or purple blossoms in acid soils, increasing the possibilities of variations with this flower.

Drying Hydrangeas

Hydrangeas, which air-dry exceptionally well, should be harvested when the sterile flowers, that is, the large ones, are dry and papery, and then hang-dried. A good way to dry hydrangeas whose flowers are still soft and supple is to use the water method, placing the stems in containers with 2 to 3 inches of water, and then letting the flowers dry slowly as the water evaporates. Even the process is ornamental, as a variety of containers can be placed in a room, creating a stair-step arrangement.

Roses

Well-suited both to upright-drying in evaporating water and to hang-drying, among other methods, roses are perhaps the most universally appealing of all flowers, fresh or dried. Their great diversity in color and form lends them to a variety of uses. Bunches of dried roses hanging from a ribbon; petals scattered across a table or in a potpourri; or whole flowers glued onto ribbons to make napkin rings or onto vellum for place cards, strung together to make garlands, or affixed to picture or mirror frames are just a few ways they can be brought into the home. With well over twenty thousand named varieties of roses, with great variation in the shapes, growth habits, and colors of the flowers and plants, the avid flowerkeeper could literally spend years experimenting with drying different varieties.

The tall, pointed buds of today's popular modern hybrid tea and floribunda roses unscroll into elegant, high-pointed blooms that are completely different from the old garden roses that once reigned over the rose world. These tightly formed buds are good for projects that require stringing flowers together and, if on long stems, make lovely hanging or upright arrangements. Once three-quarters opened, the blooms display layers of evenly spaced petals.

Each year, many more new roses are introduced by breeders, while dedicated old-rose nurseries are propagating and commercializing an increasing number of once-forgotten, heirlooms. The dried results, of course, vary from rose to rose, but there are so many different varieties from which to choose and air-drying is so easily accomplished that curiosity need not be held in check. Do note, however, that most roses dry to a darker color while whites and creams may take on a slightly buff tint.

Drying Roses

Roses of all kinds should be harvested when the flowers are in bud with two or three petals beginning to unfurl, or when the blooms are one-half to three-quarters open. If full-blown roses are harvested for air-drying, the petals will fall. They are excellent to harvest for their petals, however, because all of them will be fully developed, unlike the blooms not yet completely open.

To gather roses in bundles, allow 5 to 6 stems for most single blooms, although if they are small buds, up to a dozen stems will work. Remove the lower leaves, keeping 3 to 5 of the upper ones for a more natural look. These can always be removed later if you decide you want to use the dried roses in a mixed arrangement. Floribunda roses are best dried by the single stem. Fasten the roses with a rubber band or twine about 2 inches from the stem end, to allow air circulation around the flower heads. Attach the bundles to a hook and hang them to dry on a rack or a stretched wire.

To dry roses in evaporating water, harvest the roses as for hang-drying, then fill a container or vase one-quarter full of water. Place 6 to 10 single stems in the container, being sure no leaves are in the water. The important thing is that there be plenty of air circulation among the flower heads. Put the container in a warm, dry, dark place. The roses will develop a natural movement and grace as they dry, with their heads slightly nodding and the blooms partially opened, a different effect from hang-dried roses.

I like to dry entire bouquets with fifteen to twenty stems of all different kinds of roses, especially the mauve, palest lavender, tan, and cream ones along with those in shades of ivory and faint blush pink. I remove all the leaves, tie the stems together with ribbon, cut them to an even length, and put them in a container in a dry, dark, place. Alternatively, I fill a vase one-half full with water and put it in a window that receives direct sun. As the water evaporates and the bouquet dries, the roses fade to soft shades of peach, buff, sienna, and dusty violet.

Corsages, flowered wedding crowns, and small nosegays can be left on a table in a warm, dark room to dry. Once dried, they can be stored in a memory box, perhaps with a note describing the event or occasion when they were worn.

Rose Hip Wreath

A rose hip wreath makes a festive winter wreath to decorate a door, a gate, a dining room mirror or table. Rose hips, which are the seed pods of roses, develop after the bloom is over from blossoms left on the shrub. The pods, however, vary greatly among the different types and varieties of roses. Some roses produce very few hips, while others, such as *Rosa rugosa*, produce abundantly. In general, the most prolific producers of hips are the wild roses and the older types that predate the now-popular hybrid tea roses.

To make a rose hip wreath, select 3 or 4 rose canes with their hips, each about 3 feet long. Choose a relatively thornless variety, with hips that grow every 4 to 6 inches along the cane. Twist a cane into a circle and wire the ends together with a piece of uncoated floral wire. (You will need wire snips for cutting the wire.) Take a second cane and position it on the wired circle 3 or 4 inches from where the first circle started. Attach the second cane to the first, fastening it at the beginning, middle, and end, making an overlying circle. Continue with the remaining branches. Place the wreath on a rack in a warm, dark place with circulating air to dry.

Sunflowers and Zinnias

Sunflowers, especially those varieties that have fully developed fleshy heads, such as the classic, large disk types, are best dried upright on racks, allowing for maximum air circulation. The thick, spongy heads may take several weeks to dry. The smaller-disk sunflowers, particularly the side stems of such branching sunflowers as the colorful 'Autumn Beauty' and 'Evening Sun' or the golden yellow types, dry quite well using the hang-drying method.

Unlike many flowers whose primary purpose is decorative, the sunflower's most important use worldwide is as a source of vegetable oil, and secondarily as food both for people and for birds. Because of their economic importance, sunflowers have been the subject of plant breeding for many years and most of the production fields, even the ornamentals, are now hybrid varieties.

Many of the sunflowers lately appearing in florists' shops and green-market flower stalls are hybrids developed by the Japanese seed industry for the floral trade. Most sunflowers shed copious amounts of pollen, which is not a desirable trait for cut flowers used in displays. The most recently released hybrids are male-sterile plants, so while the flowers open brightly, they produce almost no pollen.

Most of the hybrids are *Helianthus annuus* and have yellow or gold multiple-ray petals surrounding a center disk of brown or golden green. The disk is large in comparison to the outside ray petals, resembling the proportions of the common giant sunflower. The flowers bloom on single stalks of a uniform height, generally four to five feet, and are suited for winter hothouse production and for field production during the temperate months.

Currently, the sunflowers in shades of rusty brown, dark red, golden brown, reddish pink, and bronze are for the most part not hybrids, but rather the result of breeding selections of branching, open-pollinated types. (A hybrid is the offspring of a very specific fertilization made by inbreeding two parents selected for specific genetic traits, while an open-pollinated plant is the offspring of non-inbred parents, and the fertilization may be by the pollen from several similar, but not identical, male parents.) These often grow to eight feet, with the first bloom at the top of the central stalk and side shoots with smaller flowers on short to medium-long stems. The ray petals and the size of the disk varies, but generally the latter is considerably smaller relative to the band of ray petals and seems more akin to that of a black-eyed Susan than to a sunflower. These may be *H. annuus* or *H. debilis,* the so-called cucumber leaf sunflower.

Drying Sunflowers and Zinnias

To rack-dry sunflowers of all kinds, harvest them when the blooms are three-quarters open and before the seed development is apparent. Once the seeds begin to develop, the fleshy heads droop from their own weight and become larger and more pronounced, making drying time longer. Leave about 3 inches of the stalk intact. Put the stalk through the holes in the wire or mesh, with the head resting on the mesh, spacing the heads 2 or 3 inches apart.

Zinnias, especially the heavily petaled cactus and beehive types, are rack-dried in essentially the same way. Harvest when blooms are about three-quarters open, leaving 2 to 3 inches of stem intact. Put the stems through the holes in the wire or mesh, resting the head on the mesh and spacing them an inch or 2 apart. The long, curving petals of the cactus types dry and curl to make wild, exotic-looking dried flowers, which are unusual when used in wreaths or swags.

Small-headed sunflowers on thin stems are easily hang-dried. Harvest when the ray petals are three-quarters open and before the seeds have begun to develop. Leave 10 to 12 inches of stem, or more if you like, plus a few upper leaves around the flower. Group the flowers into bundles of 3 to 5 stems and fasten them with a rubber band or tightly tied twine 3 to 4 inches from the end. Attach a wire hook and hang them on a drying rack or a wire strung across the room, spacing the bundles 6 to 8 inches apart.

Oranges, Lemons, Limes, and Pomegranates

Air-drying on racks is the simplest way to dry such thick-skinned fruits as oranges, lemons, limes, and pomegranates. As the moisture from the skin evaporates, the skin will shrink and harden, sealing the pulp and seeds inside. At this point the fruits may be considered dry, even though the pulp and seeds inside may take many more months to dry completely.

Limes, in particular, dry very quickly, but their bright green exterior often turns brownish-olive as it shrinks and dries. Thin-skinned 'Meyer' lemons and 'Moro' blood oranges both have rather small amounts of pith, the white spongelike layer just beneath the skin, and thus dry more successfully than oranges and lemons with heavier skins and thicker piths. Both lemons and oranges darken as they dry, the lemon becoming mustard colored and the blood orange turning a deep copper tinged with vermilion. Pomegranates dry quite well, darkening only slightly.

Drying Fruit

Harvest lemons, limes, and oranges fully ripe and with at least ¼ inch of the stem intact. If the skin is broken, the fruit will not dry. Pomegranates may be harvested slightly underripe or fully ripe, but without any cracks or breaks in the skin.

To dry, place the whole fruits 4 to 5 inches apart on the racks and turn occasionally. Keep the drying fruits in a warm, dry area with good air circulation. They will dry in about 2 weeks.

Lemon and orange slices are often used to create wreaths, swags, gift packaging, and other decorative crafts. Usually these have been freeze-dried, a process which is discussed in chapter 3. They can also be dried in a home-dehydrator, however, following manufacturer's directions. They will not be as hard and stiff as their freeze-dried counterparts, but they can be used to the same effect.

Calendula Salve

Calendula *(Calendula officinalis)* is notable both for its color and its medicinal qualities. It is believed by some people to have antibacterial properties and is used in salves or ointments for cuts, scrapes, and burns. It does make a wonderfully soothing salve. Making the salve requires two steps: first, oil is infused with the petals and then the oil is mixed with shaved beeswax. You will need 1 cup dried calendula petals, 1 to 1½ cups almond, sunflower, olive, or other light vegetable oil, 6 ounces of beeswax, and about 1 teaspoon tincture of benzoin (available at pharmacies).

First, grind the calendula petals in an electric coffee grinder, spice mill, or a blender, or crush them in a mortar with a pestle. Transfer to a clean, dry glass jar with a tight-fitting lid and pour the oil over them to cover. Fasten the lid and keep the jar in a very warm place, such as a kitchen, for at least 2 weeks. Do not place it in direct sunlight. Every day or so, shake the jar to mix the oil and the petals. As the oil becomes infused with the calendula, it will become fragrant and turn a deep golden yellow. A quicker method of infusing the oil is to heat it in a saucepan over very low heat and add the ground petals. Leave over very low heat, uncovered, for about 2 hours.

Once the oil is infused, place a sieve lined with 2 or 3 layers of cheesecloth over a bowl. Pour the oil through the sieve and let it drip for a day or two. Finally, squeeze the cheesecloth to release any remaining oil, then discard the calendula petals.

To make the salve, grate the beeswax on the large holes of a handheld grater. Put the infused oil in a saucepan and add the beeswax. Melt over low heat, stirring often. When the wax has melted, using a metal spoon, scoop out some of mixture and allow it to firm up. If you want a firmer salve, add more beeswax to the pan. For a thinner one, add a little more oil, just a few drops at a time.

When the consistency is to your satisfaction, let the salve cool a little. Then add the tincture of benzoin. This acts as a preservative. Put the hot salve into clean, dry widemouthed tins or jars with tight-fitting lids. Let cool until firm. Then fasten the lids and store the jars in a cool, dry place or refrigerate. The salve will last about 6 months. You should have about 1½ cups.

Oven-Dried Tomatoes

A mixture of red, pink, and yellow tomatoes sliced into delicate pinwheels makes a beautiful combination to be stored in jars or clear cellophane bags that can be given as gifts at holiday time. To make about ½ to ¾ of a pound of dried tomatoes, you will need 5 to 6 pounds of fresh tomatoes.

Slice the tomatoes thinly, ¼ inch or less. Line baking sheets with aluminum foil and place the slices on them in a single layer. Put the baking sheets in an oven preheated to 150°. Drying time will be from 7 to 24 hours, depending upon the juiciness and the thickness of the tomatoes. Leave the oven door slightly ajar and bake the tomatoes until they are leathery, but not crispy or brittle. When they seem about half dried, reverse the racks from top to bottom. Check the tomatoes often during the last few hours. Very sweet tomatoes will begin to caramelize and are subject to burning, so they need your close attention. Once dried, let the tomatoes cool, then transfer them to a paper bag, glass jar, or tin and store in a cool, dry place. For decorative purposes, string the tomatoes together to make garlands or use them to decorate gift packages.

Gathering and air-drying the season's flowers, leaves, fruits, and vines to use for decorations and crafts is both easy and satisfying. Little special skill or knowledge is required to preserve them, and once dried, they can be used in ways as simple as scattering a handful of dried leaves across a table or combining a collection of dried summer roses in a bowl with bristling chestnuts or pinecones. A *bouquet d'hiver* reminiscent of Victorian times can readily be created from your store of dried grasses and flowers, combining lengths of wheat with bluish-lavender hydrangeas, for example, or sprays of winter's rose hips. A sprinkling of dried lavender or sage leaves tucked into a letter offers a memory of summer's fragrance. It is important to remember that if exposed to a moist, humid environment, these botanicals can reabsorb moisture, however, especially the more delicate ones. To protect your dried creations from taking on moisture, spray them with a floral preservative or with hair spray.

CHAPTER 2

Pressing

During their early exploration of the New World, European botanists regularly collected all manner of plants, pressing many of them promptly to preserve them for perusal back home. Thus, the act of pressing flowers has a long and important history in scientific annals. But when most people think of pressing flowers today, they view it as nothing more than a casual way to create simple mementos. Blossoms slipped between the pages of a book, and then watched over time as the petals darken with drying, will remind the presser of a showery springtime walk or a romantic moonlight dance.

FLOWERS AND LEAVES, HOWEVER, CAN BE PRESSED ON A LARGE SCALE FOR USE IN A number of decorative ways, just as the Victorians did. The thinner a flower or plant, the easier it is to press and use for craft projects. Pansies, poppies, grasses, oak and maple leaves, petals, hollyhocks, love-in-the-mist, lilac sprigs, and hydrangeas are all good candidates. Because they are basically two-dimensional, pressed flowers can be easily attached to cards and papers or mounted and then framed behind glass, just as one would a photograph or painting. Flowers and leaves can be used on their own or together to create borders around paintings or to make bands for wrapping packages. Petals can be layered onto masks to make fanciful wear for Halloween or New Year's Eve parties, or artfully arranged on lamp shades and candles. A mixture of pressed petals and leaves can be married to create your own imaginary flowers, which can then be embedded in a wax candle or in paper. Individual leaves, which have such varied colors and shapes, are especially easy and beautiful to use for crafts and decorations.

Flower pressing is an easy craft to master. Basically, a plant is placed between sheets of absorbent paper, flattened under pressure, and kept in a warm, dry location so its moisture can be absorbed by the paper. The more quickly the drying occurs, the more likely the color and form of the object will be retained. No doubt we have all slipped a flower between the pages of a book then squeezed the book back onto a shelf to apply pressure, but it is more effective to use a press, which distributes the pressure equally across the surface, and to use a combination of absorbent blotter paper and newspaper that is changed often.

Flower presses are of several designs, but the ease of changing paper is more important than the style of press. A simple press can be made with two wood rectangles, each about twelve inches by eight inches, with a long bolt through each of the four corners. The bolts are outfitted with wing nuts that can be tightened to apply pressure. In another design, this one favored by field collectors because it is lightweight, the ends are made of wood lattice around which two leather or heavy woven straps are wrapped and tightened to hold the press together and to apply pressure. A third design uses a solid horizontal base with a solid upper piece through which extends a center bolt that can be tightened down on the layered papers. A combination of heavy books or tiles and layered papers can serve the same purpose as a more formal press.

Naturally flat, relatively two-dimensional flowers and plants, such as pansies and leaves, are the easiest to press, while multipetaled, deeply three-dimensional ones, such as orchids, calla lilies, and peonies, are more difficult. Flowers and plants with thick, fleshy stems, stamens, pistils or other parts are problematic because they carry a lot of moisture that may not be absorbed quickly enough to prevent decay. Professionals often use a scalpel or razor to slice a thick stem or flower head in half, thus retaining the form and shape, but reducing the slow-to-dry mass of the fleshy part. The flowers may be pressed face up or in a one-half or three-quarter profile, depending upon the type of flower and the desired result.

Determining the moment of harvest depends upon which stage of the flowers, leaves, or grasses you want to preserve. The first small, soft-textured, apple green oak leaves picked in May as the tree leafs out will be quite different from the large, leathery, dark green leaves picked in late summer. Violets in bud, partially open, and fully open will present three distinctly different appearances, but will press equally well. In every case, it is best to harvest when there is no visible moisture.

PRESSING FLOWERS To prepare flowers or plants for pressing, first remove any visible moisture, as it slows the drying process and invites mold. Next, lay a sheet of absorbent paper, such as blotter paper, on the bottom of the press. Follow with several thicknesses of newspaper, then put the flowers or plants to be pressed onto the newspaper or onto another sheet of absorbent paper. Cover with more newspaper, then another sheet of absorbent paper. Several sets of the layered plants may be made and numerous items may be pressed at the same time. When pressing many layers, it is best to insert additional sheets of wood or heavy cardboard between each set of plants to equalize the pressure.

Put the top of the press in place and apply pressure. The flowers should be firmly held, but not crushingly tight. Keep the press in a warm, dry location, free from insects. If possible, change the newspaper twice a day and the absorbent paper daily. Check the progress of the drying, until the flowers, leaves, or grasses are crisp, when they can be removed.

Once dry, the flowers or plants may be stored in a box or other container, still between the sheets of newspaper, in a location safely away from moisture and possible insect damage.

Specialized supplies for flower pressing can be found at herbarium supply stores, which are frequently located near universities. They usually carry a variety of different weights of acid-free mounting papers made from 100 percent cotton fiber, thick blotting papers, and acid-free manila folders. Other supplies include thin paper tape—less than one-eighth inch wide—scalpels, scissors, mounting needles, linen thread, special labels, and of course, professional presses.

To mount a pressed flower or other pressed plant suitable for framing, use a sheet of acid-free cotton fiber paper to prevent deterioration and discoloration over time. Two primary mounting methods exist, one using glue and one using ties.

In the nineteenth century professional and amateur botanists alike roamed the globe searching for unusual plant specimens. Some collected the actual plants, either uprooting them or cutting specimens, most commonly drying them in portable presses. Others painted those plants they found, providing a record of their discoveries.

Nature and things natural were in fashion, and pressed plants and plein-air painting were favored activities among people from all walks of life. While would-be artists trekked off into the country, set up their easels, and painted the glowing fields and hillsides, others packed up their flower presses and headed out to gather and press grasses, flowers, and leaves.

At home, ladies of leisure gathered and pressed such flowers as pansies or roses from their gardens. The delicate results were used to adorn cards, notebooks, memory boxes, lamp shades, and picture frames for giving as gifts or for decorating their own parlors and boudoirs.

MOUNTING PRESSED FLOWERS To mount by gluing, a white glue, such as Elmer's, is commonly employed, although in the past protein-based glue made from rabbit or yak skin or animal hooves was used. Set out several thicknesses of newspaper, then make a pool of glue on them large enough to cover the surface of the plant specimen you are mounting. Carefully lay the back of the specimen in the glue, then remove it, place it on the mounting paper, and gently press it down. Dot any stems with just enough glue to cover, and secure them on either side. Set the paper aside to dry.

To mount using the tying method, arrange the plant specimen on the paper, then with a needle, pierce a set of two holes on either side of the stem. Pass linen thread through the holes and tie a knot in the back. On multi-stemmed specimens, repeat as needed to hold the specimen in place.

Garden Journal

In this modern version of the Victorian pressed-flower journal, pressed flowers are glued onto 8½-by-11-inch sheets of medium-weight paper. There is space by each flower to write journal notes about that flower. To make the cover, you will need 2 slide sleeves and 2 sheets of cardboard. Punch holes in the cardboard and journal pages to match those in the slide sleeves. Put an assortment of pressed flowers, leaves, and seeds in the slide sleeves, sewing them shut with embroidery thread so the contents will not spill out. Again, using embroidery thread, sew 1 slide sleeve onto each sheet of cardboard. Put the journal pages inside the covers and bind all together by threading ribbon through the holes and tying securely.

Pressed-Flower Cards

Greeting cards, place cards, and gift tags can be made by affixing pressed flowers singly or in a pattern onto paper. Choose medium- to heavy-weight paper, either glossy or a matte finish, depending upon your taste and purpose. Textured watercolor paper makes an interesting background, too. Using white glue and small watercolor paintbrush, spread the glue evenly over the back of the flower in a light coat, then press the flower onto the card or tag.

Pillar Candles with Pressed Flowers

Choose pillar candles of the size you want. You will need a selection of pressed flowers that are flat yet pliable, such as pansies, individual delphiniums, individual hydrangeas, or herb leaves, including lemon balm, mint, or sage. The choices should be thin, not heavy and chunky, as these can present a fire hazard. You will also need several blocks of melted paraffin and white glue. The paraffin is flammable and should never be melted over direct heat. Carefully follow the directions on page 113 on how to work with it.

Put a small dab of glue or melted paraffin on the candle and gently press the flower or leaf onto it, pressing until the wax or glue hardens and the flowers are firmly held in place. Continue until the candle is decorated the way you want it.

To keep the flowers firmly in place and to blend them with the rest of the candle, dip a 1-inch-wide paintbrush into the melted paraffin and very gently coat the entire surface of the candle. Alternatively, hold the candle by its wick and dip it directly into the melted paraffin for a few seconds, covering it completely. Lift out and allow excess paraffin to drip off. The burning candles should always be supervised.

Species Tulips

Unlike the modern hybrids, species tulips have diminutive flowers growing on stems that are commonly only six to twelve inches tall. The smallest is *Tulipa biflora,* which is a scant three inches. Species tulips are the wild tulips from which the modern hybrids were bred. Their origins lie in the arid plateaus and rocky ravines of such places as Turkistan, Baluchistan, Turkey, and the Hindu Kush. The first tulips were introduced into Europe in the sixteenth century by a Flemish emissary of the Holy Roman emperor Ferdinand I. He had been sent on a peace mission to Suleiman the Magnificent, and on his way to the sultan's capital of Constantinople, he had seen flowers growing that were unknown in Europe. He purchased some bulbs of these flowers, which were later planted in Ferdinand's palace garden.

The fame of the tulips spread, and the Europeans, especially the Dutch, became enamored of the delicate flowers. Both professionals and amateurs began to breed them in an effort to create increasingly larger and more dramatic blooms in newer colors and newer color combinations—the forerunners of today's hybridized modern tulips. The bulbs that produced these spectacular flowers became a high-priced commodity and sold for the contemporary equivalent of from three thousand to thirty thousand dollars each, thus founding the fortunes of horticultural empires and individuals alike. Bulbs were purchased by middle-class speculators who were gambling on a tulip's doubling its price in a month—which sometimes happened—permitting a sale for a tidy profit.

Tulip lust sent collectors and adventurers forth to Asia Minor, the arid Mediterranean islands, and into Central Asia, where they searched for hitherto unknown tulip species or varieties and new supplies of known ones for their breeding programs or for sale. Although the frenzy of tulip collecting, breeding, and trading—tulip mania, as it came to be called—had abated by the end of the century, the search for wild species and their discovery and classification continued well into the twentieth century, as did the rapacious collection of wild bulbs for sale in bulk to bulb purveyors. In 1987, the Dutch bulb industry, the largest in the world, voluntarily established new labeling laws, in an effort to stop the trade in wild bulbs. Other bulb producers agreed to uphold the new statutes, and now all bulbs sold by participants, which include most European countries, the United States, and the members of the British Commonwealth, must be labeled as to their origin, that is, where the bulb was propagated. Thus, any species tulips sold today by a reputable supplier will have been commercially grown and labeled as such, rather than gathered in the wild.

Of the dozens and dozens of species tulips, a number are readily available from specialty mail-order catalog sources. They may be found listed as "botanical" tulips, as well as wild and species tulips. Their colors range from shocking red to subtle shades of bronze, tinged with olive or rose. Leaves may be gray-green, bluish, or stippled with magenta. Their shapes too are varied, with some being thin and swordlike, others broad and curving, and still others are ruffled at the edges and twisted and curled. The flowers of *Tulipa turkestanica,* a plant only five inches tall, resemble clustered creamy water lilies. The hallmarks of *T. wilsoniana*, a wild tulip from Central Asia that grows to six inches, are deep red petals with a black blotch at the throat and curled twisted leaves touched with wine red. Also from Central Asia are the *T. batalinii*, tiny specimens that grow to five or six inches and bear blooms of apricot orange, bright red, soft rosy yellow, orange-suffused yellow, or bronze on stubby, upright stems. All the species tulips lend themselves to pressing, but none is more dramatic than the orange- and yellow-spider-petaled *T. acuminata*, whose thin, twisting, four-inch-long petals flatten into fascinating patterns.

Pressing Species Tulips

Species tulips make especially lovely pressed flowers and are quite unusual because of their small size and the variety of shapes among them. For best display, they should be harvested for pressing when the flowers are one-half to fully open, and the stems and leaves can be included as well. If the stems are too thick and fleshy to press easily, slice them in half lengthwise first, leaving the flowers and leaves intact. The colors of the petals may change from early to later bloom stages, so you may wish to time your harvest depending upon the hue. *T. batalinii* is an exception to the harvesting rule altogether, because its flowers stay in pointed bud form and do not fully open.

Poppies

Comprised of a diverse group of flowers, poppies are generally characterized by paper-thin, often translucent petals that make them ideal candidates for easy pressing. One of the most unusual of the poppies is the Himalayan blue poppy, *Meconopsis betonicifolia,* a sought-after garden flower throughout Europe. With the exception of the yellow or orange *M. cambrica,* the Welsh poppy, all of the Meconopsis, of which there are approximately forty species, are from the Himalayas. In the mountains they grow in four different types of habitat, forest edges, stony slopes near streams or rivers, alpine pastures, and in cliff crevices. Their colors range from pinks and whites to deep maroon, but it is the unusual brilliant cerulean petals of *M. betonicifolia* that define Himalayan poppies for most people. The Iceland poppy, *Papaver nudicale,* although considerably more common than the Himalayan blue poppy, is unusual in that the large, single-petaled, parchmentlike flowers are bright yellow or orange, as well as white, salmon, rose, and pale yellow. Its origins are in the Arctic, where it grows as a simple wildflower, but breeders have developed the many colored poppies we are able to grow today.

Most poppies are in the red, pink, and white color range, like the wild red poppies native to the fields and ravines of the Mediterranean countries from Spain to Israel, where they appear in late spring and early summer. These are the Flanders Field poppies, *P. rhoeas,* also called corn poppies, which became the symbol of the soldiers who died in World War I. Today, on Armistice Day in the United States, Veterans of Foreign Wars sell red paper poppies atop stems of twisted green wire to commemorate the many thousands of soldiers who died on the now-forgotten battlefields of Europe between 1914 and 1918.

The glow of red poppies blanketing rural wheat fields was a favorite subject of impressionist painters, most notably Claude Monet, in his *Poppy Field* and *Path in the Ile Saint-Martin, Vetheuil.* In fact, Monet was so captivated by the flowers that he gathered some from the wild and planted them in the gardens of his home at Giverny.

California poppies, *Eschscholzia californica,* make magnificent pressed flowers because of their brilliant orange color, which remains virtually undiminished once dried, and their silky soft, rounded petals, which press to a charming bell shape. The gray-green, lacy leaves are also quite beautiful and can be used to create intriguing patterns in decorative crafts.

Breeders have developed other colors, among them 'Purple Gleam', which has mauve blossoms with yellow throats; 'Dalli', with bicolored blossoms of red and yellow, and 'Thai silk', in bright pink, orange, yellow, and red, but my heart belongs to the wild poppies that turn California's hillsides golden orange in springtime. The flowers do not need to be collected from the wild, however. You can buy seed for these poppies and sow them in your garden. Kept watered, they will bloom from spring into fall, providing you with an ongoing supply of flowers for pressing.

The oriental and somniferum poppies, glorious specimens in their rich hues of scarlet, salmon, white, and pink, have heavy multipetaled heads that make them more difficult to press than the single-petaled types. Consider instead just collecting and pressing the petals and the leaves and discarding the thick, fleshly seed head. The full heads are more successfully dried flat on racks or in sand or silica gel.

Pressing Poppies

Poppies for pressing are best harvested when the flowers are one-third to three-quarters open. Fully opened flowers drop their petals quickly. After cutting, immediately sear the cut end with a flame and, unless it is going to be pressed, immediately place in water.

Pansies

Because of its naturally flat flower face, the pansy makes one of the finest of pressed decorative flowers. Pansies as we know them today, with their rounded petals, ruffled, curving, or straight margins, blotched or lined centers, myriad color combinations, and varied sizes are the result of selection and hybridizing first done in England during the early nineteenth century. Among the most active and influential hybridizers of this period were the estate gardeners, who were encouraged by their employers to create and propagate new flower varieties.

Wild pansies, or violas, called by names such as Johnny-jump-up, love-in-idleness, and heartsease, had long been a familiar and popular feature of the English countryside. The gardening craze of the nineteenth century included garden cultivation of local plants brought in from the wild. Hence the beginning of the selecting and crossbreeding of wild violas such as *Viola tricolor* and *V. lutea,* which had petals with lines radiating from the center. The breeder's goal was to create larger flowers with different color patterns. Out of this work appeared a flower whose radial lines were fused together to make a blotch, thus creating the now familiar pansy face. The new selections were further crossed and selected to the extent that, like roses and other extensively hybridized garden flowers, the parentage became obscured.

Pansies became enormously popular because they were a new bedding plant, and elaborate flower beds were experiencing a vogue in the late nineteenth century. There was a great demand for more and more varieties and colors of the small flowering plants that were used to create intricate patterns and borders in the new landscape style.

Today, pansies remain popular for beds, borders, window boxes, and container plantings, particularly in Germany and Switzerland, where certain varieties are bred to bloom in fall and into winter and others specifically for spring and summer. In both instances, large-, medium-, and small-flowered types are available. One of the largest flowered types is 'Majestic Giant', which has flowers up to four inches in diameter in shades of yellow, violet, reddish orange, and lavender with medium to small dark blotches. Large-flowered, too, is the variety 'Imperial Antique Shades', whose unusual hues of rose, salmon, yellow, and cream combinations change colors as the flower passes from bud to maturity. I especially like the wavy-petaled 'Super Chalon Giants', whose faces display lots of whiskery lines as well as large blotches on petals of rusty red, rose, crimson, violet, burgundy, and white. Other large-flowered types have blotches so big that only a small border of color appears along the edges. Although blotches are most frequently an inky color, increasingly we are seeing pansies with blotches of red, rose, and yellow. The pansy with perhaps the most unusual—some might say unnatural—color is 'Jolly Joker', which has a bright orange blotch on a deep purple background.

Small flowering pansies, violas, and sweet violets also exhibit interesting ranges of color combinations, blotches, and lines, but there are far fewer varieties of these commercially available than there are of the large-flowered pansies. Look for the old-fashioned Johnny-jump-up, for the small pure apricot pansies, butter yellow sweet violets, and *V. nigra,* also called 'Bowles Black' viola, which has deep indigo petals soft as plush.

Pressing Pansies

Pansies for pressing can be harvested any time from bud stage to fully open, depending upon the shape you want. If the stem seems particularly thick and fleshly, remove it or slice it in half, leaving intact the flower and any leaves.

Wild Grasses

No matter where one lives, wild grasses are growing nearby. They include what we often refer to as weeds, because we don't want them in our yards or gardens. Look not only to these wild grasses to dry, but also to the numerous varieties of ornamental grasses that are available either as part of a landscape or in a cutting garden. They make beautiful pressed plants, as pressing can capture the bend of the stems and the dip of the heads, animating the dried grasses with the spirit of the growing grass. Their subtle palette of earth tones, shades of green, brown, gold, and umber, make grasses less dramatic than brightly colored flowers, but their form more than compensates for their lack of showy color.

More than forty-five hundred grass species exist, and their forms range from huge plumed plants to slender stems with stiff bristles. The roadsides abound with grasses that make interesting and unusual additions to craft projects. A pressed grass stem or two might decorate the cover of a simple handmade memory book or journal or be incorporated into a more complex design around a picture frame or on a decorative box.

Pressing Grasses

Grasses are best cut for pressing when young, before the head has filled with seed, particularly if it is a variety with a large seed head. Mature wheat, for example, has a large and heavy head that will not press flat. If you want the look that only fully formed seed heads can deliver, you can harvest them, of course, but it is best to air-dry them on racks (see page 24).

Pressed Pansy Lamp Shade

A lamp shade covered with pressed flowers is reminiscent of opulent Victorian decorating with flowers, and is quite easy to make. You will need a paper lamp shade about 8 inches high and 8 inches in diameter and 60 to 70 pressed pansies. Using a glue gun or a white glue such as Elmer's, make a dot of glue on the lamp shade and gently press a pansy onto it. Repeat, overlapping the flowers, until the lamp shade is covered. You can make a regular pattern by forming a ring around the top of the shade then continuing with slightly overlapping rings until you reach the bottom, where you will make a final ring. For a random pattern, glue the pansies in a scattered pattern and then fill in the spaces. This method can be used with other pressed flowers as well, such as dogwood or hydrangea, or even with silica-dried flowers, dahlias or daisies, for example.

Pressed Flower and Clear Glass Frame

You will need a clear glass frame, which is 2 sheets of glass held together in a frame, usually with hanging hooks at the top for wire or ribbon. You will also need a selection of pressed flowers and leaves. Very flat specimens such as hydrangea, pansies, poppies, delphinium, rose and tulip petals, ivy, grape, and ginkgo leaves, as well as ferns, are good choices for this project. You will also need a photo or other flat memorabilia, such as postcards or labels, and clear tape.

Undo the glass frame and carefully clean the glass with glass cleaner to remove any streaks or dust. On a piece of paper the same size as the glass, practive laying out your design. When it pleases you, lay one piece of the glass on a plain surface or on a piece of white paper to provide a non-distracting background. Place the photo or other memorabilia where you want it, then arrange the pressed flowers around it. Carefully place the other piece of glass on top and fasten the pieces together with clear tape along the edges, where they will be hidden beneath the frame. Replace the frame according to the manufacturer's instructions. If desired, add ribbon through the hooks to hang the picture on a wall or window. NOTE: If the frame is hung in a sunny window, the flowers will fade.

Window Hanging of Pressed Leaves

This simple project is especially fun for children, as they can lay out the leaves in a pattern they like, then, with adult supervision, iron them between the sheets of waxed paper. Hang their artistic creations in a window to show them off.

Trim 2 sheets of waxed paper to the desired size. Place several layers of white paper or newsprint on an ironing board or other work surface. Heat an iron to medium-low. Place 1 sheet of waxed paper on the white paper and arrange the pressed leaves on it. Lay the other sheet of waxed paper on top, matching the edges. (They can be trimmed later.) Lay a sheet of aluminum foil over the top sheet of the waxed paper to protect the surface of the iron from the wax. Gently move the iron back and forth over the foil until the wax on the paper has warmed and the 2 sheets are stuck together, sealing the leaves in between. Remove the aluminum foil. To finish, trim the edges to even them if needed.

Pressed Leaf and Flower Masks

You will need a firm half mask, made of plain fabric or plastic, available at costume and craft suppy stores, at least 1 yard of ribbon, between 1 and 2 inches wide, and an assortment of pressed flowers and leaves. The quantity of flowers and leaves that is needed will depend upon their size. For example, a half mask will need about 16 pressed delphinium or hydrangea flowers, or about 20 pressed viburnum leaves. In order to select the size and shapes that best fit the mask, you should have at least double the amount you think you will need. Among the flowers, pansies, nigella, coreopsis, rose petals, and daisies are good choices and among the leaves, grape, maple, liquid amber, and oak.

Remove the elastic tie thread from the mask. Cut the ribbon in half and thread a length of ribbon through each tie hole, knotting the end on the inside. It is important to do this before gluing the leaves or petals, because the finished mask is somewhat fragile.

Lay the leaves or petals out in an approximate pattern, to get a sense of how they will overlap and the quantity you will need. Using a soft brush apply a thin layer of white glue to the back of a petal and press it into place. Glue the bottom ones first. Do not put glue on any parts that will extend past the edge of the mask. It may be necessary to use pieces of petals or leaves, especially around the eye holes.

FRANCIS

MARIA

LUANNE

MORGAN

Pressing flowers is a quick and easy pastime that can be quite rewarding, whether you want to keep a single souvenir of a special occasion, maintain a large collection to enjoy looking at, or decorate your home or artifacts. Gathering and pressing flowers is part of a long tradition, a tradition that fits easily into our busy contemporary lives. Little has changed over the years in the tools and techniques needed to press flowers, whether for romantic or scientific purposes. Everyone has a moment or two to slip a flower between sheets of paper and weight it with a favorite novel.

CHAPTER 3

Silver Sand–, Silica-, and Freeze-Drying

Flowers dried with silver sand, silica gel, or a mixture of borax and cornmeal look incredibly lifelike, yet have an ethereal porcelain element, retaining their original color and shape to a much greater extent than air-dried flowers. Freeze-drying, a relatively new method that requires expensive machinery, produces perfect-looking flowers, fruits, and vegetables. Of course, most amateur flowerkeepers will not have access to the costly equipment, but freeze-dried flowers can be purchased at floral supply stores if you wish to work with them.

FLOWERS DRIED USING ANY OF THESE FOUR METHODS ARE THE BEST CHOICES FOR decorative crafts where you want the flowers to look as if they are alive. They can be used to decorate boxes, using just one or two blossoms or creating a top with a solid covering, or incorporated into wreaths, made into decorative frames for photographs or mirrors, and fashioned into bands or attached to ribbon streamers. Collections of small flowers look lovely displayed in a glass box, similar to that used for a shell or insect collection. Scattered on a table among small votive candles, they look as though they were just cut. Glass lamps filled with delicate flowers in a single color are an invitation to admire them. One must use caution, however, for these methods produce particularly fragile flowers that will suffer if handled excessively.

Virtually all flowers can be dried in sand, silica, or a borax-cornmeal mixture, but these are methods especially useful for heavily petaled, full-headed flowers such as peonies, roses, dahlias, and zinnias. Fragile-petaled flowers, including daisies, hollyhocks, and larkspur, are also suitable to being dried using these media, although silica is preferred because there is less danger of the delicate petals being cut by a bit of sharp sand.

Silica, or silica gel as it is also called, is a granular desiccant made from silicon dioxide that absorbs moisture from the flower, accelerating the drying process. Sand, borax, and cornmeal are not desiccants and using them serves only to hold the flowers in position as they gradually dry. The flowers are placed in a container, face up, face down, or sideways, depending upon the type of flower, then surrounded and covered by the drying medium, whose fine grains hold and support the flowers and each petal in its natural form as the flower dries.

An essential difference between using sand and using a desiccant is the timing factor. Flowers in silica gel must be checked frequently. If left too long in the desiccant, they will become brittle, shatter, and deteriorate, while flowers in sand or borax and cornmeal combinations are not at risk. Generally speaking, flowers in silica will dry within a day or two or up to a week, those in borax-cornmeal combinations within two weeks, and those in sand only in about two weeks, but there remain numerous variables. Small flowers with light, papery petals will dry more quickly than heavy-headed, multipetaled flowers. Moisture content varies from flower to flower, from one type of growing condition to another. Drying times will also vary according to climate and season. The best insurance is to experiment to determine the length of time needed for drying specific flowers under your particular conditions.

DRYING IN SAND AND BORAX-CORNMEAL Silver sand was commonly used for drying flowers in the nineteenth century and earlier. Despite its glamorous name, it was simply clean, fine sand from riverbeds or beaches from which all traces of silt or other contaminants had been removed by multiple siftings and rinsings. Any good quality, common sand can be used for drying, but the finer and the cleaner the sand, the less likely it is to damage the flower petals. Coarse sand has sharp edges that nick and pock the petals, as does debris such as bits of broken stems, splinters, or shells.

Although sand is out of fashion today, superseded by the quicker-acting silica gel, it has several virtues to recommend it. There is virtually no danger of overdrying and shattering brittle petals, nor does it leave behind traces of powder on the flowers as do silica gel and borax mixtures. Sand is also particularly useful for drying flowers with multiple layers of cupped petals, as the minuscule grains of sand can be sifted into the thickets of petals to ensure every bit of the flower is reach, which is more difficult to do with the larger-grained silica.

Borax and cornmeal are often used together in combinations varying from half and half to two parts borax to one part cornmeal. The varying proportions have more to do with availability and personal preference than with drying effectiveness. The white powder left behind on the flower petals should be dusted off with a water-color brush or soft cotton.

Silica can be purchased at craft stores. The type used for flower drying usually contains granules that change color to indicate the silica is dry. When it has absorbed too much moisture to be effective, the granules turn red. The red silica must be dried out in an oven according to the manufacturer's directions. This is easily done, usually by placing the silica in a slow oven. Once the moisture-marking granules have changed from red back to blue, in one to two hours, depending upon the amount of moisture that was absorbed, the silica is ready to use again.

Flowers to be dried in silica, sand, or a borax-cornmeal mixture may be harvested at any time when the flowers are between one-quarter to fully open and no moisture is visible. Buds may be harvested as well, but large, thick buds may be difficult to dry successfully. Leaves and stems may be left attached, or removed.

Although sand, silica gel, and borax-cornmeal mixtures all have different properties, the method for using them to dry flowers is nearly the same. The primary difference is that silica requires an airtight container to prevent it from absorbing airborne moisture, while the others use open containers to allow for maximum air circulation to aid in drying.

Most flowers are dried faceup, with or without the stem. Some schools of thought recommend removing the stems before drying and replacing them with wires, while others suggest removing the stems, drying them separately, and wiring the flower head with a short piece of wire to be used later to reattach the original or another stem. Finally, there are advocates of leaving the stem attached. The determining factor seems to be a matter of personal style, the eventual use for the dried flowers, and the size of the containers being used.

For faceup drying in sand, fill the container with enough sand or other medium to allow the stem to be placed upright, yet leaving enough headroom in the container to cover the flower completely with the sand. Shoe boxes are good choices for smaller flowers, but for larger ones cardboard cartons are better. The cartons will need to be covered, but they don't need to be airtight.

If you are drying more than one flower, make sure the petals aren't touching. Since sand flows so readily, a good way to get into the deepest curls and crevices of the flower is to let the sand flow from your hand so that it builds a "wall" about the flower. Then gently tip the container; letting the sand flow across and through the petals and find its own level. Continue until only the top of the flower is exposed, then dribble sand through your hand across the top. Finish by covering with at least an inch of sand. Alternatively, scoop out a hole in the sand large enough to hold the flower, place the flower in the hole and drizzle in sand to fill the hole and cover the flower, gently shifting the container from side to side to allow the sand to flow. Do not continue shifting once the top of the flower is covered. Continue covering until there is at least a one-inch layer of sand over the top of the flower.

For horizontal positioning in sand, scoop out a hole and lay the flower into it. Drizzle the sand and shift the container as described above. For drying face down, make a small mound of sand in the bottom of the container, place the flower face down on top of it, and drizzle sand around the flower until there is at least a one-inch layer of sand covering it. Use borax-cornmeal mixtures the same as you would sand. Sometimes a little extra assistance from a small paintbrush or spoon is needed to get the mixture deep into the heart of the flower, as these two substances don't flow as easily as sand.

Once the flowers are covered, place the container in a warm, dry location. Check the drying flowers every few days by gently brushing aside the drying medium until a few petals are exposed. Once they feel papery to the touch, expose the flowers one at a time by tipping the container and carefully pouring off the drying medium while one hand supports the dried flower until it is freed.

To store the flowers, carefully wrap them in paper and put them into a box. Place the box in a dry location. Alternatively, leave the dried flowers on the surface of the sand or borax-cornmeal mixture with the stems pushed down, and keep in a dry, dark location.

DRYING IN SILICA To dry flowers in silica gel, you must use an airtight container. Because of the fine particles, always wear a dust mask when working with silica. Plastic storage boxes or large plastic kitchenware containers are good choices. Place the flowers upright and drizzle the silica gel over them until they are just barely covered. Cover tightly. The next day, look to see to what extent the flowers have dried. Those with light, somewhat papery petals like love-in-a-mist will tend to dry quite quickly. If the petals feel dry, but still supple to the touch, gently slip a fork under them or use your fingers to lift them. Place them on the surface of the silica, cover tightly with the lid, and leave to dry for another day. Ideally the petals should be no longer supple, but completely dry, although not crackling dry. Again, the best rule is to experiment, always checking to make sure the flowers are not getting too dried. Once dried, dust away the powdery residue with a watercolor paintbrush and store the flowers in a covered box in a dry location. If you are planning to use your silica-dried flowers near or with food, it is essential they be brushed completely free of any silica powder, as it can make you extremely ill if ingested.

FREEZE-DRYING While freeze-drying produces results similar to those achieved with silica, sand, and borax-cornmeal, it yields products that are even more lifelike. Numerous types of flowers, fruits, and vegetables can be freeze-dried, leaving the original seemingly unchanged other than becoming slightly more intense in color and greatly reduced in weight. A large, freeze-dried dinner-plate-size dahlia, its brilliant purple-and-white petals looking lush and succulent, has not more weight in the hand than a dandelion puff.

In other methods of drying flowers, the water in the flowers is a liquid when it is removed from the cells of the plant, and the cell walls rupture in the process. The change in appearance between the fresh and the dried is caused by the collapse of the cell walls and the consequent loss of pigment. In freeze-drying, however, the cell walls stay relatively intact because the water is removed as a vapor, which passes through the cell walls without damaging them.

Freeze-drying, unlike other methods of flower drying or preserving, requires a serious investment in a specialized piece of equipment, a freeze-dryer. Freeze-dryers have two airtight cylindrical chambers, one large and one small. The flowers are placed on racks in the larger chamber (a medium-size machine may hold up to three thousand blossoms), the cylinders sealed, and the temperature set to –20 degrees Fahrenheit in the larger chamber, and to –70 degrees Fahrenheit in the smaller chamber, the ice bank. The machine's vacuum pump then begins to remove the air from the chambers. In an atmosphere with greatly reduced pressure, water in a solid state—the ice in the flowers—will change to a vapor without becoming a liquid. Consequently, the moisture in the flowers moves a vapor into the surrounding atmosphere, where it is drawn to the other much colder chamber and frozen again into a solid, becoming a block of ice. Successive blocks are removed until there is no longer any discernible moisture present, then the machine is shut off and the flowers removed. The length of time to accomplish this process varies from several days to several weeks, depending upon what is being dried. Large vegetables such as artichokes, cauliflower, and eggplants take considerably more time than pansies.

Because freeze-dried flowers will reabsorb moisture, they must have a post-drying treatment to seal them and protect them. Different types of sprays and dips that accomplish this are available and some have an ultra-violet inhibiting agent to preserve the color of the bloom as well as to seal its surface.

Freeze-dried flowers make excellent candidates for crafts, and like flowers dried with sand, silica, and borax-cornmeal mixtures, require careful handling because of their fragility. Once made into a wreath or used in another decorative way, however, they are long lasting.

VICTORIAN PASTIMES

అ

Drying flowers and leaves in silver sand was a popular pastime with Victorian ladies. Magazines and books of the period advised their readers on techniques, choices of flowers, and how to use the dried flowers for decoration, ornamenting everything from lamp shades and notebooks to hat bands. At the City Garden Museum in London, a place card is on display in a glass case. The card, with a name still faintly legible, is presumably from a long-ago dinner party. It is decorated with a dried pansy, and the identifying label says simply, "Place card with pansy dried in silver sand."

Decorated Box

Choose a box that you like and cover it with brightly colored tissue or other paper. Using a glue gun, glue a single dried flower to the top. Alternatively, still using the glue gun, glue flowers in a scattered pattern over the top and the sides of the box. You might use all the same flowers, daisies for example, or mix them, using different sizes and colors. Pressed flowers may be used as well.

Old Garden Roses

Roses dried in sand, silica gel, or in a borax-sand mixture retain their colors and shape and look extremely life-like. Old garden roses, currently enjoying a renaissance among floral stylists and gardeners alike, are frequently characterized by rather flat or rounded buds that open to variations of flat-topped cups of densely packed petals often organized in quadrants around a tight button center. 'Souvenir de la Malmaison', an old Bourbon rose that bears large, heavily fragrant blooms of blushed ivory cream, and 'William Lobb', an equally fragrant moss rose whose midsize blooms are deepest magenta, are good examples of the old rose shape, as are the cabbage roses *(Rosa centifolia),* which were so often depicted in Flemish paintings of the seventeenth and eighteenth centuries. The old garden roses, with the exception of the tea roses, have a color range limited to shades of pink, magenta, purple, and white. The teas, which also have
the pinks, come in light yellow and buff as well. Since the old garden roses retain their intense colors and their fragrance after drying, they are my favorites to collect and dry for potpourris and for sprinkling into letters. All the old roses are noted for the intensity and depth of their fragrance, an attribute that some tea roses lack.

The now-familiar rose colors of bright yellow, orange, apricot, and all their hues and shades did not appear in garden roses until after the development of the hybrid tea rose. French rose breeder Joseph Pernet-Ducher succeeded in introducing the bright yellow of the wild species rose, *R. foetida* 'Persiana', into the hybrid tea roses in the late 1880s. Some of the early hybrid teas from the late nineteenth and early twentieth centuries have unusual and subtle colors and shadings that reflect their close proximity to the tea roses and the early introduction of yellow. If you are growing these or can locate them, it is rewarding to experiment with drying them, as the results are distinctly different from the hybrid teas of the later period.

Floribunda roses, which were developed in the early part of the twentieth century, provide an entire bouquet of roses on a single stem, unlike the hybrid tea, which ideally produces a single bloom per stem. For the most part, the buds are like those of hybrid teas, but there is a great deal of variation among the flower shapes and colors, a variety that exists nowhere else in rosedom. Delicate mauves that are tinged with lavender-brown, coffee cream fading to pink, amber yellow with a brownish cast, russet browns, tan touched with pink and yellow are all found among the floribundas. Look for 'Lavender Pinocchio', 'Julia's Rose', 'Brownie', and 'Café', which are as unusual dried as they are fresh. Floribunda roses are best dried on single stems, as grouping the multiheaded stems together makes for too large a bundle, which will inhibit the air circulation needed for drying. Once dried, however, they shrink, so several of these stems in a vase or other container with make an impressive display.

It is in the English roses introduced since the mid-1960s by rose breeder David Austin that one finds blossoms that exhibit the fragrance and the bud and flower shapes of the old garden roses, but that have the color range of both the modern and the traditional. Deep crimson, blush pink, buff yellow, glowing apricot, fragile pinks, and shades of salmon and white are found in the large flat, double and semidouble cupped flowers that bloom throughout the season. Some have a single bloom per stem, while others have multiple blooms.

Wreath of Dried Garden Roses

This is one of the most beautiful, yet one of the simplest, wreaths you can make. Once completed, it can be hung on a wall or over a mirror, or used as an elegant table decoration. The roses can be chosen to complement your color scheme.

You will need a 10½-inch Styrofoam wreath form, about ½ inch thick; 25 to 30 silica-, sand-, or borax-dried or freeze-dried roses of different sizes; 4 or 5 6- to 8-inch lengths of fresh bay or other shapely leaves; a hot-glue gun; and floral wire. If the wreath form is thicker, use a serrated knife to cut it to the correct size.

Lay the wreath on a flat surface, then arrange the flowers around it to decide on your pattern. As you attach the flowers, you may find more are needed to fill a gap here and there.

Using a glue gun, apply a small amount of glue to the back of a flower and press it gently to the wreath form, being sure to cover all exposed surfaces of the wreath form, including the inside. For extra preserving, spray the wreath lightly all over with hair spray or a floral fixative. Do not place the wreath in direct sunlight or the flowers will fade.

Wreath of Dried Summer Flowers

You will need a grapevine wreath about 12 inches in diameter; a hot glue gun; an assortment of silica-, sand-, or borax-cornmeal-dried flowers, such as dahlias, hollyhocks, daisies, delphinium, lisianthus, zinnia and gladioli; plus floral wire and 4 or 5 6- to 8-inch lengths of fresh bay or other shapely leaves. Lay the grapevine wreath on a flat surface then arrange the flowers around it to decide on your pattern. As you attach the flowers, you may find more are needed to fill a gap here and there.

Using the hot glue gun, apply a small amount to the back of a flower and press it gently to the wreath form. Repeat until all the flowers and leaves are attached. Let the glue dry, then fasten a piece of floral wire to the back of the wreath so it may be hung. Use hair spray or a floral fixative for extra preserving, and keep away from direct sunlight.

Zinnias

Available in an exuberant range of colors, from primary red and yellow to delicate shades of mauve, dusty rose, lavender, and cream, and on to bright pink, carmine, and orange, zinnias darken only slightly when dried in sand, silica, or a borax-cornmeal mixture. Like the narcissus, the zinnia has paper-thin petals and a hollow stem and dries quite quickly, and the flower head, while often large, is not fleshy and spongy. Many zinnia varieties—'Beehive' and 'Lilliput', for example—have dense, multilayered petals, however, and it is difficult to ensure that even very fine sand can reach all the way to their petal base. Less tightly petaled, and therefore easier to preserve, are the 'Giant Cactus' zinnias with pointed petals and the 'Giant Double', which have rounded, dahlialike petals. The petals are attached to a flower head that increases in size as the flowers mature, opening up space between the petals.

Zinnias are members of the *Compositae* family. The family name derives from the flower heads, which are a composite of many small flowers or florets. If you look carefully at the heart of a zinnia, for example, you will see a collection of tiny, yellow florets. Zinnias are among the quickest and easiest of all summer flowers to grow and need only mediocre ground, water, and sun—the same requirements as the other simple-to-grow members of the *Compositae* family: sunflowers, cosmos, and bachelor's buttons. Their large seeds are easily handled, germinate within a week when planted into warm soil, and generally produce flowers in sixty days. They are a good choice for an easy-to-grow cutting garden and an abundant source of flowers for drying.

Picture Frame Bordered with Dried Zinnias

Covering a wooden or metal picture frame with dried zinnias creates a playful home for favorite photos or collectibles, such as seed packets. You will need an inexpensive picture frame about 9-inches square and about 20 silica-, borax-, or freeze-dried zinnias of different sizes. Position the zinnias around the frame as desired. Place dots of glue on the frame and gently press the flowers onto the glue.

For drying in sand, silica, or a borax-cornmeal mixture, harvest zinnias when three-quarters to almost fully open. Once dried, petals may drop from overly mature flower heads. Position the flowers stem down with the bloom facing upward.

Peonies

When dried in silica, sand, or a borax-cornmeal mixture, peonies are among the most spectacular of dried flowers, because their color, shapes, and texture are so clearly preserved. When air-dried, the petals wrinkle and crumple like crepe paper, which, although a nice effect, is quite different from that achieved with silica, sand, or a borax mixture. Once dried, they make beautiful displays simply arranged in the base of a glass-bottomed lamp, where their loveliness can be enjoyed every day over the years.

Among the early breeders and promoters of peonies were the Kelways of Langport in Somerset, England. In 1874, they were considered the largest growers of peonies in England and offered over 850 different varieties for sale, many of them scented. The introduction of *Paeonia lactiflora (albiflora),* a fragrant peony whose origins are in Tibet, China, and Siberia, allowed hybridizers to create peonies with rich, delicate fragrance similar to that of roses. This new attribute, plus a greater and greater size and variety of form and coloring, increased the interest in peonies both in England and abroad. Huge specimens were shown at the popular flower and garden shows of the late nineteenth and early twentieth centuries, where peonies, being considered exotic, were a popular exhibitor's plant. Amateur and professional breeders and horticulturists all competed in the shows, showing off the achievements of their garden.

Most of today's available garden or herbaceous peonies are derived in some way from *P. lactiflora* hybrids, but there has been such extensive breeding over the last hundred years that the newer varieties may not be fragrant. Peony trees, on the other hand, are hybrids not from *P. lactiflora,* but from another species, *P. suffruticosa,* and may or may not have a fragrance. Peony trees are capable of producing enormous blooms with heads so heavy they bend their branches with their weight and these, when successfully dried, are truly a stunning sight.

Drying Peonies

Peonies are well-suited to drying in silica, sand, or a borax-cornmeal mixture, but the process requires patience, especially with the fluffy double types, to ensure that the granules or grains of the drying medium reach to the tightly packed base of the flower head. Silica seems to work the best for this, as the flowers finish drying to perfection once placed on top of the silica in the final stage.

Harvest peonies for drying in silica, sand, or borax-cornmeal mixtures when they are three-quarters to fully open, and position them stem down, bloom up.

Flowers preserved in sand, silica, or borax-cornmeal mixtures or by freeze-drying have the most vibrant colors and the most realistic, lifelike appearances of all the preserved flowers. Luscious garden roses in a variety of brilliant colors and shapes marry to make a wreath or a swag. Fanciful flowers, like daisies and zinnias, perhaps interspersed with brightly colored fall leaves, can be used to decorate gift boxes and picture frames. Narcissus, paper thin and delicate, bring a breath of spring to a winter table. And, more extraordinary of all, silica-, sand-, borax-, or freeze-dried roses affixed to a moss-covered pillow creates a charming decoration for a favorite chair, whether your own or a friend's.

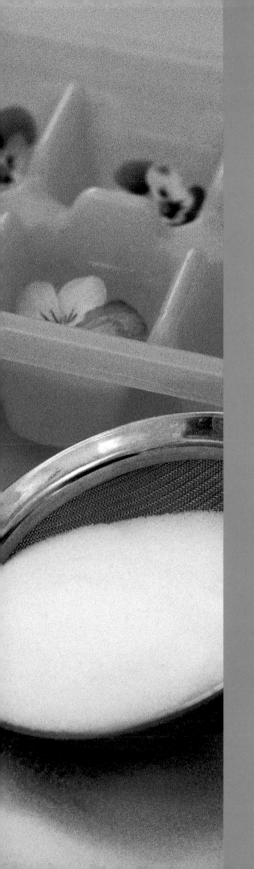

CHAPTER 4

Waxing, Sugaring, and Freezing in Ice

Waxing, sugaring, and freezing in ice are all highly successful methods for preserving flowers and other plants. Waxing and sugaring coat blossoms, leaves, or fruits with a covering that seals them from moisture. Freezing them in ice is fleeting, lasting only as long as the ice, but it is a dramatic way to showcase them.

*T*HIS CHAPTER CELEBRATES THREE VERY EASY AND QUICK METHODS OF KEEPING flowers—waxing, sugaring, and preserving in ice. No special rules of harvesting are needed, because the flowers are held in suspension, encased by wax, sugar, or ice, and their petals cannot fall or their shapes deteriorate. Because the beauty of the fresh flowers is captured only for a few hours or a few days, they should be used for special occasions where their ephemeral loveliness, like the occasion, lasts only for the moment.

These are such easy, near-instant ways to preserve flowers, and the results are so beautiful and unusual, we truly encourage you to plunge into the experience. Unlike air-drying, pressing, or preserving flowers in silica or sand, which, while easy to do, nevertheless require time and patience to produce the end result, the gratification of the processes in this chapter are virtually immediate.

Each of these very different methods produces results that are beautiful additions to everyday life. Fruits and leaves cloaked in sugar make sparkling garnishes for drinks, cakes, and other sweets. Sugared mint leaves add a dashing garnish to mint juleps, as do sugared borage blossoms to old-fashioned lemonade. A cluster of sugared grapes and grape leaves or a handful of whole sugared cherries is an eye-catching ornament for a chocolate cake. Sugared rose petals and violets, which last for months, are classic decorations, but pansies, orange blossoms, and day lilies are other edible flowers that can also be sugared. For an elegant centerpiece, combine bunches of sugared grapes with a few sugared peaches, nectarines, and plums and tuck in sugared ivy leaves. All kinds of wonderful flowers, fruits, leaves, and shrub branches can be frozen in ice of all shapes. Especially spectacular is ice frozen in the shape of a champagne bucket with branches of flowering quince or ferns frozen into the ice. Single perfect poppies can be frozen into individual small rounds to ornament a punch bowl. Tiny violas can be frozen into pebbles of ice to chill sparkling water. Waxed flowers can be used to create wreaths and candle holders, or to decorate gifts. Waxed fruits, when displayed on cake stands or in bowls and interspersed with waxed flowers and leaves, make stunning centerpieces.

Waxed Flowers and Magnolia Leaves

In the early part of the twentieth century, when the horrors of World War I were fresh in people's minds and those of World War II were not yet imagined, every year on May 31 wreaths were placed on gravestones and the steps of city halls and hung on civic statues in towns and cities across the United States to honor those killed in The Great War. The occasion, called Memorial Day, commemorated the day in 1918 that the armistice was signed between the members of the triumphant Triple Entente and the defeated Triple Alliance.

Most wreaths were made of preserved magnolia leaves dyed very dark and then decorated with waxed flowers. The preservation of the leaves was done in three different locations — Evergreen, Alabama; Besen, Illinois; and San Francisco, California — by five different companies. Three of the companies were headed by men of Danish origins, two by men of German origin, all using a preserving technique first developed by I. G. Farben, a huge German chemical company.

First the leaves were dipped in big vats full of hot red, brown, or green dye. From there they were scooped out and put into other vats with a chemical solution that fixed the color and kept the leaves supple. Finally they were transferred to wooden crates that were then racked, slightly tilted, to allow the leaves to drain and dry.

When the leaves were dry enough, the boxes were taken to sorting rooms and graded by hand by large crews, mostly of women. The good leaves, those that were adequately dry and supple like fine leather, were packed into heavy cartons or wooden shipping crates. The wooden crates were packed with fifty pounds of leaves, the cartons packed with either five or ten pounds. The preserved leaves were then shipped to florists small and large, coast to coast, where they were made into wreaths and decorated with waxed flowers and red, white, and blue ribbons.

WAXING Wax may be applied to many fresh and dried flowers and leaves and some fruits as well. Essentially, fresh or dried flowers are dipped into melted paraffin to seal them, thus protecting them from decay. It is extremely easy and quick to do, even for the complete novice, and it is enormously satisfying to produce such stunning results so quickly.

Flowers that have first been dried will last indefinitely, but fresh flowers may last only a few days. After that, they begin to brown and discolor. Waxy flowers such as orange blossoms and hyacinth last longer than more fragile roses and tulips. Flowers that have been dried in silica gel (see page 89) or freeze-dried (see page 90) and have a natural appearance are easier to wax than the air dried flowers and look more lifelike because they have a smooth, rather than wrinkly surface. Since they are already dried, they will last indefinitely when preserved in wax. Pressed leaves and pressed flowers (see page 51) wax beautifully and are long lasting as well.

Good flowers to choose fresh for waxing are orange blossoms, grape hyacinths, baby roses and tea roses, short-cupped narcissuses, small sunflowers, wild onions, and brodieias. These will all last at least a week and sometimes up to a month. Pink and yellow calla lilies look magnificent waxed, but last only a few days, as do the larger tea roses. In general, white flowers tend to show damage and decay and are best avoided.

Fresh flowers that are dense and heavy, such as old-fashioned heavy-petaled roses, peonies, and cactus dahlias are not good candidates because they tend to take on so much wax that the petals lose their distinctive shape and become stuck together. If these flowers are dried, however, they will wax much more successfully, especially if you use toothpicks or skewers to separate the petals a bit while they are still supple with the warm wax.

Among the best of the fruits to wax are pomegranates, grapes, figs, cherries, persimmons, limes, oranges, and lemons. These will last a month or more. Radishes, carrots, and asparagus wax well, but will last only a week or so.

A much more widely practiced technique during the nineteenth and early twentieth century than today, waxing provided still-life arrangements for tabletops and mantels in homes across Europe and North America. Generally the arrangements were placed under glass bells or cloches to protect them from dust and insects. When kept thus and away from heat and direct sunlight, the waxed flowers would keep for years. Waxed flowers continued to be used until the 1950s, when an extensive variety of readily available air-dried flowers, many of them imported from Europe and Asia, supplanted them in popularity.

THE WAXING PROCESS The process of waxing is quite simple, but a number of things will ensure that the procedure goes smoothly. Paraffin is the wax used and it may be purchased at hardware stores and in the canning and baking sections of supermarkets, generally in packages of four blocks. To melt enough paraffin to dip and coat six to eight medium-sized flowers, put two blocks of paraffin in a heatproof container, such as a coffee can, reserved for this purpose. Because paraffin is quite flammable, do not put the paraffin container over direct heat. Instead, place the container in a pan of simmering water and stir the paraffin as it melts. When it has liquefied and is clear, it is ready to use. Ideally, the wax should be just warm enough to stay in this state. If it is very hot, it can damage the fresh flowers, although this is not a problem if you are using dried blooms.

Place a large bowl of cold water next to the waxing area. If you dunk a flower or other plant immediately into the cold water after it is removed from the wax, the water will set the wax and give it a sheen rather than a matte finish. Have enough flowers on hand to experiment until you have the look you want. Finally, set out a wire rack with newspaper or waxed paper beneath to hold the finished flowers.

Waxed Radish and Wild Onion Wreath

To create this splendid wreath you will need a 10-inch twisted grapevine wreath, 4 or 5 bunches of radishes with their leaves intact, about 2 dozen or so stems of wild onions in bloom, about 16 to 20 10-inch lengths of fresh bay leaves or other greenery, green-coated floral wire, small wire cutters, plus the waxing equipment described on page 114. Cut 12 pieces of wire, each about 5 inches long. The radishes and wild onions are assembled in bundles before they are dipped and wired to the wreath, as wiring is very difficult if attempted later.

Separate the radishes and wash and dry them, removing any damaged leaves. Bend the wires in half. Place 2 or 3 radishes and a sprig of wild onion together, resting it in the bend of one of the pieces of wire. Gently but firmly twist the wire to secure the bundle. Do not bind too tightly, or the stems of the radishes are liable to break off. Set aside. When all the bundles are made, prepare the paraffin and container of cold water and put out a sheet of waxed paper large enough to accommodate the bundles.

When the paraffin is ready, hold the bundle by the wire and dip it into the wax, just enough to cover the radishes and onion. Remove and submerge the bundle immediately in the cold water. Remove from the water and set aside on the waxed paper. Repeat until all the bundles are waxed.

If desired, omit the cold water step and instead let the radishes cool on the waxed paper, then dip them again in the wax, return to the waxed paper and let cool.

To assemble the wreath, use floral wire to attach the bay leaves to the wreath, covering it. then, using the floral wire, attach the bundles of waxed radishes and wild onions to the wreath.

Narcissus

Narcissuses, a group of flowering bulbs that includes daffodils and jonquils, are highly varied in size, shape, and color, and many of them are notable for their intense fragrance. With their distinct shapes and firm, rather waxy texture, they, like hyacinth, another spring bulb, make excellent candidates for waxing.

Those with cups longer than their petals are generally referred to as daffodils or trumpet daffodils. 'King Alfred', a sturdy yellow daffodil introduced in 1899, remains one of the most popular today, though the numerous new pink-trumpeted or bicolored types are more glamorous. The pink of the trumpets may be salmon, apricot, coral, or rose and either pastel or intensely colored. 'General Patton' has a frilly yellow trumpet, but bright white petals. 'Royal Scarlet' has a reddish-orange trumpet and large, deep yellow petals.

Large- and small-cupped narcissuses form another category. Their cups are shorter than the trumpet cups of the daffodils. Literally dozens and dozens of different varieties within this category are available, a situation that makes a search for flowers of unusual color combinations and shapes quite fruitful. 'Barrett Browning' has cups of saffron orange and creamy ivory petals, and 'Ambergate', one of my particular favorites, has amber petals surrounding a large cup brilliantly colored in carnelian red. 'Petit Four' not only has a frilly double cup, but the cup itself is a lush apricot-pink surrounded by large white petals.

Other categories include narcissuses with ruffled doubled centers, reflexing petals, those that bloom in dangling clusters, those with upright clusters, and some in miniature size. The 'Pheasant's Eye' is one of the oldest narcissuses in cultivation and is said to have a fragrance so intense and sweet that a dozen blooms will overwhelm an ordinary-sized room. Of equal fragrance is the 'Chinese Sacred Lily', whose spiced nutmeg and mace scent wafts on the air to create fragrance-laden pools. Both these narcissuses have small orange cups and ivory petals, but however nice it would be, the fragrance does not linger when the flowers have been waxed, so enjoy their heady scent before dipping the flowers in wax.

Wreath of Waxed Spring Flowers

For this luscious wreath of flowers you will need a 10-inch twisted grapevine wreath, about 40 to 50 fresh flowers, such as grape hyacinth (muscari), hyacinth, short-cup daffodils, miniature roses, paperwhite narcissus, or tea roses, 16 to 20 10-inch lengths of fresh bay leaves or other greenery, green-coated floral wire, small wire cutters, plus the equipment for waxing described on page 114. Cut the flower stems to the desired length, about 2 or 3 inches. Cut a piece of floral wire for each flower, at least 8 inches long or longer if the wreath is quite thick. It is better to cut the pieces too long and trim later if necessary.

Bend a piece of wire in half, place the stem of the flower in the bend, then carefully wrap the wire around the flower's stem, leaving a length of wire free on either side. Do not let the wire cut into the stem and this can cause the stem to weaken. Repeat until all the flowers are done.

Prepare the paraffin (see page 114). When the paraffin is ready, quickly dip the flower head into the melted paraffin to cover where the wire holds the flower. For a glossy finish, immediately plunge the dipped flower into cold water, then turn it around and dip the stem up to and slightly overlapping the previous dip line, immediately plunge the dipped stem into cold water. If a matte finish is preferred, allow the flower to cool slightly on its own before dipping the stem end. Set aside and allow the flower to cool before dipping again, if desired. The more dips, the more waxy and less colorful the flowers will appear. Continue until all the flowers are dipped and cooled.

Using the floral wire, attach the bay leaves or other greenery to the wreath to cover it. Decide how the flowers will be arranged. to attach them, gently bend open the wire holding the flower and then nestle it against the wreath, wrapping the wire around to the back of the grapevines and securing them. Clip off any extra wire. Repeat until all the flowers are attached. If the wax cracks severely at the wire junction where it attaches to the flower, use an old brush to gently apply melted paraffin over the cracks to reseal. Attach a wire to the back of the wreath to hang it, or use it as a table centerpiece with candles.

Waxed Flower & Fruit Centerpiece

Depending on the size of your table, you will need a number of 1- to 3-feet-long branches of fresh bay leaves or other seasonal greenery, small apples, paperwhite narcissus flowers, and white or cream colored pillar candles of varying heights, with saucers. You will also need bamboo skewers, a small, inexpensive brush, and kitchen tongs. This arrangement could also be made with other fruits, such as citrus and citrus leaves, pomegranates, cherries, pears, or star fruits. Other flowers, like daffodils, roses, passion flowers, or hyacinth, could be used and even vegetables such as including radishes, asparagus, baby carrots, beets, and squash.

Prepare the paraffin as directed on page 114. To wax the apples, pierce the underside of the apple with a skewer just enough to hold the apple securely. Plunge the apple into the melted paraffin, then remove it hold it in the air to cool slightly. For a glossy finish on the wax, dip the apple briefly into a bowl of cold water. Repeat the dipping until you have reached the desired thickness, remember that the thicker the wax, the less the apple's color shines through. Gently remove the apple from the skewer, and using a small brush, apply a small amount of wax over the hole, sealing the apple entirely. (NOTE: It is impossible to remove the wax from the brush.)

To wax the flowers, first trim the stems to about 3 inches below the flower. Holding the stems about halfway down their length with kitchen tongs. Plunge the flowers into the melted paraffin just to the tip of the tongs. For a glossy finish, dip the flower in cold water immediatley after removing it from the paraffin. Hold the flower upside down and allow it to cool slightly, then reverse it in the tongs, gently holding it just below the head. Be careful not to crack the wax finish. Dip the stem into the paraffin until it slightly overlaps the previous dip line. Repeat this process until you have achieved the desired finish and thickness.

To assemble the centerpiece, place a protective cloth or waxed paper in the center of the table. Arrange the greenery loosely, then place the pillar candles on their saucers among the leaves, taking care that the leaves do not reach too closely to the candle sides. Arrange the apples and flowers around the greenery and leaves. This arrangement should last 2 or 3 days before the flowers begin to brown. The apples will last longer, about 10 days.

SUGARING Sugaring flowers and fruits is easily done with egg whites, a paintbrush, and superfine sugar. This was a popular method of presenting fruits at Victorian teas and dinner parties. Sometimes the fruits to be sugared had been previously steeped in sweetened brandy, and biting through their sugared crust to the sweet-fire taste of the fruit beneath was a well-appreciated delight. Tiny edible flowers such as violets, rose petals, and small leaves such as those of mint were also sugared, and these were served either as candies for nibbling or used to garnish cakes and other sweets. The less convoluted, ribbed, or heavily petaled the flower to be sugar and the more two dimensional it or the fruit, the greater the success of the finished product, especially for amateurs.

For most sugaring projects, 3 egg whites and 1 to 2 cups of superfine sugar will be adequate. Place the egg whites in a bowl, and using a fork or whisk, beat them until frothy but not stiff. Put the sugar in a bowl, and lay out several pieces of waxed paper.

Using your fingers, tweezers or tongs, depending upon the size of the flower or fruit you are sugaring, dip a single flower, flower petal, or piece of fruit into the egg whites, covering thoroughly. Place the coated object in the sugar bowl, then spoon sugar over it to cover. Carefully lift up and shake off the excess sugar. Place on the waxed paper to dry. If the object seems to be picking up too much egg white and becoming too heavily sugared, use a small brush instead to paint on the egg whites. If the egg whites lose their frothiness, beat them again. Let the objects stand overnight in a dry location.

Sugared flowers or flower petals and leaves dry very well, and can be stored in an airtight container and kept in a cool, dark place for up to 6 months. Sugared fruits, such as cherries, grapes, kumquats, and plums will form a crisp crust when dry, but will not keep longer than a day or two. They should be used within 36 hours of sugaring for the best effect.

Miniature Roses

Baby roses are ideal for sugaring and using as edible decorations for cakes and cookies, because of their small size and delicate shapes. Defined as small rose bushes with small leaves and flowers in proportion to the size of the plant, miniature roses have become exceedingly popular in the last thirty years, particularly in the United States, and extensive breeding has gone into creating the hundreds of different varieties. The plants, including climbers, are generally between twelve and eighteen inches. Specimens that are larger than these miniatures but still smaller than a full-size bush are likely to be classified as patio roses or ground cover roses.

The modern introduction of the miniature rose began with a bright pink rose growing in a pot on a windowsill in Switzerland. It was owned by a Colonel Roulet, whose friend Henri Correvan was a breeder of roses. The colonel gave Correvan a cutting, from which Correvan propagated the miniature roses that he introduced to the market in 1920, naming the rose after his friend, 'Rouletii'. It was an American rose breeder, Ralph Moore, however, who working initially with 'Rouletii', is universally acknowledged as having been the major influence on the breeding and popularizing of miniature roses.

Their small plant size and repeated and extended blooming period, along with the myriad nuances of colors they exhibit, have made these roses increasingly appreciated for their intrinsic value, not just as a passing fads. As tiny replicas of larger roses, the miniatures display not only the characteristic high-pointed bud shapes of the modern roses, but also the cupped, quartered, and reflexed petals characteristics of the old roses. The flowers may be multi- or single-petaled, the bushes thorny or thornless, the blooms in candelabra clusters and sprays or atop single stems. Some, like 'Daniela' and 'Renny', have pointed petals that resemble those of water lilies, while others have softly rounded petals with tips that curl back like those of 'Rainbow's End'. 'Dresden Doll', a tiny moss rose, has petals that form a perfect cup. 'Oriental Simplex' is a single petal rose with five shockingly scarlet petals, the bases of which are tipped with gold and surround a cluster of long, golden stamens. 'Pinstripe' and 'Stars 'n' Stripes' are variegated shades of white, red, and pink, while 'Pandemonium', another of the many variegated roses, is bright red and yellow. In short, the miniatures encompass nearly all the possibilities available in full-size roses.

Sugared Cherries or Flowers

To sugar a dozen cherries (with stems) or flowers such as pansies, you will need 3 egg whites and 1 cup superfine sugar. Place the egg whites in a bowl and, using a fork or whisk, beat them until frothy but not stiff. Put the cherries on a piece of waxed paper with their stems up and place flowers face up. Put the sugar in a bowl.

Using your fingers, hold a cherry or flower by its stem and dip it into the egg whites. Let drip for a moment over the bowl, then put the cherry or flower in the bowl of sugar and spoon more sugar over it. Carefully lift up the cherry or flower and shake off the excess sugar. Return it to the waxed paper to dry. If the cherries or flower seem to be picking up too much egg white and becoming too heavily sugared, use a small brush to paint on the egg whites. If the egg whites lose their frothiness, beat them again. Let the cherries or flowers stand overnight in a dry location. Use the cherries within 24 hours. Use flat flowers such as pansies within 3 days.

FREEZING IN ICE Almost any flowers, herbs, fruits, leaves, or small branches can be frozen in ice, capturing the essence of the season in an elegant and shimmering arrangement. Because the ice is at its most beautiful when clear, use distilled water, rather than tap water. Tap water may have impurities that will result in cloudy ice.

There are many possibilities. Single flowers or single fruits, such as grapes or blackberries, can be put into ice-cube trays, frozen, and used to garnish drinks. Fanciful ice molds, such as swans or medallions, can be purchased at craft or restaurant supply stores and flowers frozen in them. Simple cooking pans, such as loaf pans or angel food cake pans can be used as well. In fact, any container that will hold water can be pressed into service, including milk cartons, yogurt cartons, and other common containers. Once frozen the floral ice block can be floated in a punch bowl, placed in a container to chill bottled drinks, or used as decoration on a buffet table.

In preparing frozen flowers, you will need to take several steps. Once the water is added, some of the flowers, leaves, or other plants will float to the surface. To position and distribute them throughout the container, first place them in the container, then partially freeze the water. Using a long wooden skewer and toothpicks, push the leaves or flowers down into the soft ice to position them as desired and return to the freezer. This may need to be repeated several times to achieve the desired effect.

To unmold, wrap a hot towel around the mold for a minute or two, just to loosen the ice, or dip the mold in hot, but not boiling, water, then turn or slip out the ice block. If you have used a milk carton or similar container, you can tear or cut away the mold and discard it.

Frozen Rose Ice Bucket

An ice bucket with brilliantly colored roses captured inside creates a gorgeous, ephemeral centerpiece for a special occasion. You will need a very clean 8- to 10-gallon plastic or other nonrusting bucket and an empty 2-liter plastic bottle with unridged sides. You will also need about 5 gallons of distilled water, a dozen or so fresh yellow roses, and some fresh rose leaves.

Using scissors or a razor, cut off the top of the soda bottle. Put a few rocks in the plastic bottle to weight it in place once the water is poured into the bucket. Place the weighted bottle in the center of the bucket. Place the roses and leaves around the bottle, between the bottle and the bucket. Pour distilled water between the bottle and the bucket, filling nearly to the top of the bottle. Place in the freezer and freeze until a thin layer of ice has formed, about an hour or so. Remove from the freezer and, using a long wooden skewer or similar utensil, push any roses or leaves that have surfaced back down under the ice. Return to the freezer and freeze for another hour. Remove and again push down the roses and leaves with the skewer, dispersing them in the icing water. Return to the freezer and freeze until the water has frozen into a solid block of ice, about 24 hours.

To unmold, wrap the bucket with hot, damp towels for a minute or two, let stand for just a few seconds in a basin of hot water. Place a folded towel on a baking sheet and place it, towel down, on top of the bucket. Holding the baking sheet and bucket in both hands, invert and lift off the bucket. (This is best accomplished with two people.) Once unmolded, the ice bucket can be returned to the freezer for up to 24 hours before using.

To use the bucket, place it on a tray to collect the water as it melts. Slip a bottle of chilled Champagne, white wine, or other beverage into the rose-strewn bucket.

Frozen Vodka in a Frozen Fern Block

With the vodka bottle literally frozen into a fern-filled block of ice, there is no question that the vodka you pour will be truly chilled.

You will need a fifth (750 ml) of 100-proof vodka, a clean, square half-gallon milk carton, 8 to 10 fresh fern fronds in different sizes, and about ½ gallon of distilled water. This is not suitable for wine, other low-alcohol beverages, sodas, or fruit juices, as these will freeze and can explode.

Place the vodka bottle in the center of the milk carton. Slip the ferns between the bottle and the inside of the milk carton and pour in the distilled water to reach nearly to the top. Place in the freezer and freeze until a thin layer of ice has formed, about an hour or so. Remove from the freezer and, using a long wooden skewer or similar utensil, push any fern fronds that have surfaced back down under the ice. Return to the freezer and freeze for another hour. Remove and again push down the fern fronds with the skewer, dispersing them in the icing water. Return to the freezer until the water has frozen into a solid block of ice, about 24 hours.

To unmold, tear away the carton and discard it. Rinse the frozen block to remove any bits of clinging cardboard. The frozen vodka and fern block can be returned to the freezer and kept there for up to 24 hours before serving.

To use, place the bottle and its ice block on a tray to collect the water as it melts. Have a towel ready to use for pouring, as the block is heavy and needs to be held carefully while pouring.

Freezing in ice, waxing, and sugaring are all simple ways not only to preserve flowers, but also to show them off in a surprising way. The end results in every case are glamorous, yet so easy to do that even novices can execute the crafts with great success. Within a short time, you can find yourself with a beautiful tray of sugared fruits for a dinner party or a centerpiece display, or a collection of waxed flowers to use for table decorations, wreaths, or to decorate gifts. You can also readily make beautiful flower-filled blocks of ice for garnishing punch bowls, individual cubes for chilling drinks, and even buckets for cooling full bottles.

The art of flowerkeeping has so much to offer, from the pleasures of collecting flowers, leaves, grasses, even nuts and seeds, to the satisfaction of the processes. Whether air-drying or pressing flowers, drying them in silica, sand, or borax and cornmeal, you will have preserved and transformed their beauty into something lasting. with just a little imagination and time, your preserved flowers can be used to create gifts, adornments, and decorations, from picture frames to lamp shades. Preserved, even briefly, in wax, sugar, or ice, flowers create a special mood for a festive event, when champagne is poured from a frozen still life of roses, sugared pansies do tea time cookies, and waxen wreaths of spring flowers glow among a table of candles.

FLOWERKEEPING TOOLS

For many of the craft ideas in this book, it is a good idea to keep a few simple tools on hand. A strainer is helpful when working with salves, such as Calendula Salve on page 44. Q-tips, white glue, and kitchen tongs are useful when dipping flowers in wax. A dust mask should always be worn when working with silica gel. Waxed paper has dozens of uses, and a small supply of grapevine wreath forms means you can readily prepare a wreath of dried or waxed flowers. Of course, the project pantry needs scissors. Ice trays are a quick way to freeze edible flowers and herbs into pretty cubes, and an assortment of inexpensive brushes can be used for dusting off flowers dried in silica, sand, or borax-cornmeal, as well as for applying glue. A hot-glue gun is essential for attaching larger flowers to wreaths, boxes, or other decorative items, and there is always a use for different weights of floral wire. Twine for tying bunches of leaves and flowers, an air-tight container for silica, and a can of melted paraffin and skewers for waxing projects complete the basic craft pantry.

LUNA

ACKNOWLEDGMENTS

We wish to thank the many people who generously gave of their time and talents to make this book possible.

Our deepest thanks to Teresa Retzlaff, Kathryn's studio manager and production assistant, whose enthusiasm and creativity are responsible for so many of the craft projects. Her craft research and craft expertise were beyond our expectations, and we gratefully thank her for all of the time, energy, and support she has given to this book.

Thank you to Caroline Kopp and Anthony Gamboa for their assistance with photography. Their skillful efficiency helped us to accomplish a tremendous amount in a very short time.

Many thanks to stylist Sarah Dawson, who contributed her resourcefulness and wonderful touch with flowers to this book. Her willingness to take on any project, no matter how obscure, with high spirits and creativity is most appreciated.

Thank you to Robert Retzlaff and Cynthia Welsh, Kathryn and Ralph Retzlaff, Judy Dawson and Helie Robertson for generously allowing us to plunder their gardens in search of flowers and fruits to preserve.

A special thank-you from Georgeanne to all of the people who helped so generously with background research on the preserving horticulture and history of flowers: Dr. Allan Armitage of the University of Georgia at Athens; Sally Ferguson of the Bulb Research Center in Booklyn, New York; Knut Nielson Jr. of Evergreen, Alabama; Van Oium at Northstar Freeze-dry Manufacturing in Minnesota; Kieft Seeds, Holland; Dr. Bruce Bartholomew and Janet Jones of the Academy of Science, San Francisco, California; Augustin Thieffery, formerly of Vilmorin Seeds, France; David Jeffery, formerly of Unwins Seeds, England.

Thank you to Lupe Coleman, Luanne Blaich, Kristin Jakob, Wendy Addison at Theatre of Dreams, Ray Giacopazzi at Hillcrest Farms, Suzi Elgin at Kisetsu, Toni Elling at Meadowsweets, Amanda Marcus, Judy Blair, Caroline Kopp, Eric Schwab and Charlotte Kimball for allowing us to use and photograph their beautiful keepsakes and creations.

Thank you to Gretchen Scoble for her exquisite book design and for her willingness to allow us to participate in the design process. The book has her wonderful sense of color and design from beginning to end.

Thank you to Kirsty Melville, Lorena Jones, and Jason Rath, our team of editors at Ten Speed Press, for trusting our vision and making the book possible.

A special thank-you to Sharon Silva and Jim Schrupp for their adept and thoughtful editing.

❧

BIBLIOGRAPHY

Armitage, Allan M. *Specialty Cut Flowers.*
Portland, Oregon: Varsity Press/Timber Press, 1993.

Austin, David. *Shrub Roses and Climbing Roses.* Woodbridge
Suffolk, U.K.: Antique Collectors' Club Ltd., 1993.

Bullivant, Elizabeth. *Dried Fresh Flowers from Your Garden.*
London: Pellman Books/Stephen Greene Press, 1989.

Clayton-Payne, Andrew. *Flower Gardens of Victorian England.*
New York: Rizzoli International, 1988.

Commercial Field Production of Cut and Dried Flowers. A national
symposium sponsored by the Center for Alternative Crops
and Products, University of Minnesota, and the American
Society of Horticultural Science, December 6–8, 1988.

Davies, Jennifer. *The Victorian Flower Garden.*
London: BBC Books, 1991.

—*The Victorian Kitchen Garden.* London: BBC Books, 1988.

Elliott, Charles. "Tibet's Great Blue Poppy."
Horticulture, Vol. LXXII, No. 5, May 1994.

Green, Mindy. *Calendula.* New Canaan,
Connecticut: Keats Publishing, Inc., 1998.

Hortus Third Dictionary. New York: Macmillan, 1976.

Kleinman, Kathryn and Michaele Thunen. *Souvenirs.*
San Francisco: Harper San Francisco, 1994.

Lawrence, George H.M., editor. "America's Garden Legacy: a
taste for pleasure." The Pennsylvania Horticultural Society,
Philadelphia, Pennsylvania, 1978.

McCann, Sean. *Miniature Roses, Their Care and Cultivation.*
Harrisburg, Pennsylvania: Stackpole Books, 1991.

Frederick McGourty, editor, "Dried Flower Designs," *Brooklyn
Botanic Garden Record,* Vol. 30, No. 3, #76. Brooklyn
Botanic Gardens, Inc., Brooklyn, New York. 1974.

Meunier, Christiane. *Lavandes et Lavandins.*
Aix-en-Provence, France: Edisud, 1985.

Middleton, Dorothy. *Victorian Lady Travellers.* Dutton, New
York, New York. Reprint with new introduction.
Chicago: Academy Chicago Publishers, 1982.

Moore, Ralph S. *The Breeding and Development of Modern Moss
Roses.* Visalia, California: Moore-Sequoia, 1978.

Phillips, Roger and Martyn Rix. *The Random House Guide to
Roses.* New York: Random House, 1988.

"Proceedings of the 4th National Conference on Specialty Cut
Flowers." Cleveland, Ohio, Association of Specialty Cut
Flower Growers, Inc., November 1–4, 1991.

Robinson, William. *The English Flower Garden,* 15th edition.
London: J. Murray, 1933. U.K. reprint. A Ngaere Macray
Book, New York: The Amaryllis Press, 1984.

Vilmorin-Andrieux et Cie. 1894. *Les Fleurs de Pleine Terre.*
1989 reprint. Les Editions, 1900.

RESOURCES

The Bone Room, Berkeley, CA

The Paper Pile, San Anselmo, CA

Tale of the Yak, Berkeley, CA

Meadowsweets, Middleburgh, NY

Kisetsu, San Anslemo, CA

Theatre of Dreams, Port Costa, CA

Hillcrest Farms, Petaluma, CA

Katrina Roselle Patisserie, Berkeley, CA

INDEX